The Fruits of Virtue

The Fruits of Virtue

Finding Peace and Plenty
in a Chaotic World

Making the Case for Living a Principle-Centered Life

Michael J. Harris, Ph.D.

Contents

Acknowledgements

Inspiration at times is like the wind: [it] bloweth where it listeth, and thou hearest the sound thereof, but canst not tell whence it cometh, and whither it goeth" (John 3:8).

We can certainly put ourselves in places where our minds are more receptive to inspiration, but that's only part of the story. The message must be relevant and offered up at the right time! I believe now is the time for a message on virtuous living.

I was out riding my bike in the cool of the morning when I received flashes of inspiration to write this book and what it should contain. I was excited to finish my ride and start this project. This all happened in the beginning of the pandemic, which at this time was only six months ago.

I credit my Heavenly Father for any and all of the enlightenment I received. It certainly comes in all sorts of ways and places.

For Joy, my wife, who never complained with the time needed for this project—in reading, writing, and putting it all together.

For the mostly silent and unknown heroes, who along with their stories, offer up demonstrable virtues and wonderful templates for living.

Preface

What is truth?

The Lord has said, "truth is knowledge of things as they are, and as they were, and as they are to come" (Doctrine and Covenants 93:24). There are principles and truths that have always existed; they are not arbitrary.

Much of life has shades of gray, but there are also absolutes: gravity, night and day, good and evil. We know them when we see them; it's almost an inherent thing. Trying to legislate wrong things as right or deny truth because of popular opinion will never change objective reality.

For several generations and in an ever-increasing way, there has been a movement away from established moral truths that for centuries were universally accepted. Some have taken the position that their actions are merely expressions of their individual rights. They refer to these positions as being "their truth." It's as if they are entitled to write and follow their own owner's manual for the universe . . . and of course, it never works.

When any of us make a personal discovery, gain more insight, or profit from our own life experiences, it is a beautiful thing. These events are often life-changing and accelerate our personal growth and appreciation for life. But those experiences can't undo the larger reality of *natural law.* (We will visit this shortly.)

"The largest growing religious organization is that of Unaffiliated; the largest growing political movement is Unaffiliated. Since 1999, the suicide rate has increased thirty percent. Since 2011 the teenage suicide rate has increased seventy percent. College depression rates have doubled in the last ten years. These are a lot of the people who may be searching for truth. They are likely lonely, isolated and very afraid." (David Brooks, "Finding the Road to Character," BYU Forum, 22 October 2019).

I am not suggesting that all these folks are not good or moral people. We all suffer; we all struggle. There is real depression, real confusion, and devastating life challenges! There is addiction and other habits that are harmful to us and others. Any one of us can lose our way for a wide variety of reasons. This is not about blame. It is about how we can find our way out of, or through, hard things. I'm suggesting another paradigm for living, one that brings real meaning and clarity.

Is there objective truth? If so, do we care about it anymore? And where do we find it?

Jesus said, "And ye shall know the truth and the truth shall make you free." Does having real freedom mean being able to do whatever one wants? We need freedom that supports an internal liberation, one that preserves a course where we discover our true self and purpose, and one that invites us to use our gifts in blessing the lives of others. I think this is the best definition of freedom.

Mark Manson has said, "In order to live the life you truly want to live, you have to first be clear about what you truly value because that's where your emotional energy will be directed."

So, finding what we value and testing it against tried and true principles will provide valuable information.

True principles, though not always easy to follow, will bear fruit—the fruit of peace and plenty. Peace in this context means peace of mind and conscience, as well as the peace of being comforted. Plenty in this instance means to have abundance, though not necessarily in wealth. When we learn or relearn, and seek to follow these cosmic principles, we will reap the rewards that are sure and true.

For there are many "blinded by the subtle craftiness of men . . . who are only kept from the truth because they know not where to find it" (Doctrine and Covenants 123:12).

I think we all desire real peace and happiness. There's a course we can follow that brings internally-felt blessings and still preserves our authentic, individual self. Though we'll all be challenged through our own Pride Cycle, wanting to do what *we* want and in *our* own way (chapter five), it's how we learn and grow and ultimately refine ourselves.

It's my sincere desire to make a case for life's true ethics, and advocate for their pursuit. It's woven into our spiritual DNA—our souls. These principles are logical, intuitive and natural, and they bring about peace and plenty.

Introduction

When the founding fathers assembled in search of the keys for a robust, enduring government, they looked to some of the greatest thinkers of all time. By studying their ideas, these men hoped to find a common set of principles that would lead toward a document that would uphold the dignity and rights of humankind. This had never been accomplished by man in any lasting way.

The Founders were children of transgenerational colonists whose roots were European (mostly English), and who came from places where monarchies had ruled the day. How could they uncover and organize a set of working ideas and principles that would promote freedom, while at the same time restrain the slippery slope of autocracy or dictatorship? It was a monumental task.

They studied the writings of Polybius, Cicero, Thomas Hooker, Coke, Montesquieu, Blackstone, John Locke, and Adam Smith. They studied the writings of the Bible, particularly the Old Testament, as well as the teachings of Jesus. Though some did not belong to any specific Christian denomination, they collectively shared a respect and admiration for divine wisdom.

Their readings and study spanned Greek, Roman, Anglo-Saxon, European, and English history. They wanted to extract the most important ideas from religion, politics, and economics that would contribute and advance this new society. There was a lot of data to mine and refine.

They wanted certain things, such as the people to remain free, a nation that would have autonomy, and for a government that would be limited in scope and influence. They realized when people were enlightened by true principles, they could govern themselves accordingly. A vital key for success was a charter or constitution established on true and enduring principles. They would ideally need leaders (being imperfect themselves) who would try to live and govern by these same principles.

They knew for a freedom-loving and freedom-keeping society the people would need to be a moral people, as the best societies were ones where the people governed themselves.

Today, the government is run mostly by an elite group who move back and forth from the private sector (often from Wall Street) into bureaucratic positions. Increasingly, those who are elected seem to serve for lengthy periods and often lose touch as true public servants. Many never knew or have forgotten who a citizen-leader is—someone who serves for a term or two and returns to the private sector. We need people who seek to serve us and not a lifestyle that serves their own interests. The vast majority of Americans support term limits. American citizens want leaders who inspire and possess real character. This should be the template. But I digress.

As the Founders identified, discussed, and debated the wealth of knowledge found in the great minds of the world and of scripture, they collectively began to see a common set of truths—principles that were both unifying and liberating to all of humankind. These are referred to as natural law.

These laws were first recognized and written about by the Stoics in the third century BC. Stoicism is a philosophy based on personal ethics and using one's mind to understand the world. They believed that virtue was the basic good, being seen as more important that one's health, wealth, or pleasure, and it placed a greater emphasis on behavior rather than words. To live a good life was to learn the rules of nature as everything was rooted there.

Some of the Framers subscribed to these ideas but held an overriding belief in a Supreme Being as well. They clearly stated that "we hold these truths to be self-evident, that all men are created equal, that they are endowed by their Creator with certain unalienable Rights, that among these are Life, Liberty and the pursuit of Happiness."

One of the biggest concerns of the Founders (as well as other colonists) was whether they would be moral enough to create a society that would work for them. Benjamin Franklin wrote, "Only a virtuous people are capable of freedom. As nations become corrupt and vicious, they have more need of masters" (Smyth, *Writings of Benjamin Franklin,* 9:569).

George Washington added that the Constitution would only survive "so long as there shall remain any virtue in the body of the people" (Saul K. Padover, ed., The Washington Papers; New York: Harper and Brothers, 1955, p. 244).

James Madison said, "Is there no virtue among us? . . . to suppose that any form of government will secure liberty or happiness, without any virtue in the people, is a chimerical [impossible] idea. (Quoted in Jonathon Elliot, ed., *The Debates in the Several State Conventions on the Adoption of the Federal Constitution,* 5 Vols.; Philadelphia: J P Lippincott Company, 1901, 3:36–37).

Finally, Thomas Jefferson stated, "Virtue is not hereditary" (Ford, *Writings of Thomas Jefferson,* p. 227). His suggestion was that all people must learn of virtue and earn it. Virtue is not a permanent thing in our natures; it must be practiced and internalized.

In their time, the Founders saw that the people would learn virtues from three basic sources: the home, the school, and the church.

Where do we learn about virtues today?

Many if not most of the principles in this book are not politically correct; therefore, they're not acceptable for public discussion. In their time, these virtues were the common curriculum at home and in the public square. Leaders and statesmen talked of God and His mercy: "With a firm reliance on the protection of divine Providence"; "appealing to the Supreme Judge of the world for the rectitude of our intentions."

So, what does all this mean?

It means that ultimate freedom is found in possessing and preserving the power to choose. Outward or external freedom is found in the activities of a free society where liberties are assured. To think, feel, and speak; to act as long as we don't infringe on others; to aspire toward a goal and succeed or fail; to worship; to move about and assemble. These and others are the freedoms we desire for ourselves and our posterity, but they must be safeguarded if they are to endure.

All the Founders serve as role models for principle-centered living. The freedoms they helped establish cost them dearly. Of the fifty-six signers of the Declaration of Independence:

> Nine signers died of wounds or hardships during the Revolutionary War. Five were captured or imprisoned, in some cases with brutal treatment. The wives, sons and daughters of others were killed, jailed, mistreated, persecuted or left penniless. One was driven from his wife's deathbed and lost all his children. The houses of twelve signers were burned to the ground. Seventeen lost everything they owned.
>
> Every signer was labeled as a traitor; everyone was hunted. Most were driven into flight; most were at one time or another barred from their families or their homes. Most were offered immunity, freedom, rewards, their property, or the lives and release of loved ones [if they would] . . . break their pledged word or to take the King's protection. Their fortunes were forfeit, but their honor was not. No signer defected or changed his stand throughout the darkest hours (Shelby Cullom Davis, delivered at Windsor Castle; Diana Davis Spencer Foundation). https://ddsfoundation.org/our-sacred-honor/s

These facts speak volumes. Their lives are a testimony. They demonstrated that commitment to a cause and strength of character will come when one lives by longstanding virtues and principles. They are heroes and show that we all have the capacity to live a little better, to live on a little higher plane.

Preservation of freedom is strongly associated with virtue and how human beings or a society abide by these precepts. Internal freedom, that which brings peace of mind and conscience and joy, comes through living a virtuous life.

"Where the Spirit of the Lord is, there is liberty" (2 Corinthians 3:17; see also Alma 61:15).

This suggests to me that the Creator is even more visible and heartfelt when we abide by His natural laws.

For many centuries natural law was accepted as both an undergirding and a cover by providing guiding principles for living. These laws provided protection from the elements (the winds of progressive change).

Why did our founding fathers seem to have a great interest and respect for natural law, which often is associated as traditional values or morality? Have we progressed so far, solved so many societal ills, that natural law is no longer relevant? Are we so sophisticated, so self-sufficient, that we no longer need or deny the existence of a Supreme Being from which natural law emanates?

We can't turn back the hands of time, for ourselves or the world in which we live. The world is more than an assortment of nations and their governments. It's ultimately about the people and the quality of life they can have. Living in accordance with natural law is tried and true. It bears the fruits of peace and plenty and increases harmony among all people.

This book is about the importance of embracing virtues. (There are many others I've not addressed.) These virtues are the universal truths for living and being. They require effort and practice but always bear fruit. Natural law comes from God our Creator. The design is His— it's eternal and it works. As humans we are flawed and finite. We can't improve upon these divine principles. The way to fully discover them is to learn about and practice them.

We should tread lightly when we seek to create our own golden calf.

Paul, an ancient apostle from the New Testament, encouraged us that

"Brethren, whatsoever things are true, whatsoever things are honest, whatsoever things are just, whatsoever things are pure, whatsoever things are lovely, whatsoever things are of good report; if there be any virtue, and if there be any praise, think on these things" (Philippians 4:8).

As we study and learn, then live by true principles (virtues), we will enjoy the high life!

"Our virtues are like crystals hidden in rocks. No man shall find them by any soft ways, but by the hammer and by fire." (Henry Ward Beecher, Proverbs from Plymouth Pulpit).

The Virtues of Belief

Hope, Faith, Wisdom

The virtues of belief demonstrate the power of our mind and heart—that if we can only believe, anything is possible. After realizing how hope and faith bring us through difficult things, we become anchored with milestones of certainty. With the passage of time, experience, and reflection, faith becomes knowledge and knowledge wisdom.

Chapter 1

Hope

"Live, then, and be happy, beloved children of my heart, and never forget that until the day God will deign [condescend] to reveal the future to man, all human wisdom is contained in these two words—'Wait and hope.'
—Alexandre Dumas

What Is Hope?

Hope has been defined as a feeling of expectation; a desire for a certain thing to happen; an attitude for better things to come.

What does hope mean to you?

What do you hope for?

What do you want or more importantly need in your life right now?

I really like how Richard Rohr describes hope. He says, "The theological virtue of hope is the patient and trustful willingness to live without closure, without resolution, and still be content and even happy because our satisfaction is now at another level, and our source is beyond ourselves."[1]

It's this kind of hope that fills one with light and is sustained by a higher power, the true source of hope. It has been said that hope is a precursor to faith. Paul in Hebrews said, "Faith is the substance of things hoped for."

Faith thus comes about as a result of hope. Much of life is filled with challenge, uncertainty, hardship. Without hope we could not envision a better tomorrow or expect to find solutions to our problems today.

An interesting story is told of the famous preacher Robert Robinson (1726–1791). After dissenting from the Church of England, he went on to become a well-known Baptist minister, hymnist, and author. He's best known for the hymn "Come, Thou Fount of Every Blessing" and for a lifelong study of the history of Christianity and the doctrine of baptism. As a preacher he may have railed on others to repent, but he also offered hope for those trying to find salvation.

The story states that one day while he was riding in a stagecoach, a lady asked him what he thought of the hymn she was humming. He responded, "Madam, I am the poor unhappy man who wrote that hymn many years ago, and I would give a thousand worlds, if I had them, to enjoy the feelings I had then."[2]

It seems he may have lost hope.

In the final period of his life, Robinson spent time with Joseph Priestley, an infamous political and theological radical of the late eighteenth century. Priestley and his fellow Unitarians who denied the deity of Christ were quick to claim Robinson as one of their adherents.

Perhaps we should feel some sympathy for Robinson, as in his later years he seemed broken. He was seriously ill, both physically and mentally, when he died in 1791. His congregates reported that his sermons became unintelligible. Some said he'd become insane. His seventeen year-old daughter Julie died in 1787, and he never seemed to recover from her death. He faced financial ruin and nearly went to debtors' prison. Many of his so-called friends turned against him.[3]

Some of the lyrics from his most famous hymn read:

Come, Thou fount of every blessing,
Tune my heart to sing Thy grace;
Streams of mercy, never ceasing,
Call for songs of loudest praise.
Teach me some melodious sonnet,
Sung by flaming tongues above.
Praise the mount! I'm fixed upon it,
Mount of Thy redeeming love.

Sorrowing I shall be in spirit,
Till released from flesh and sin,
Yet from what I do inherit,
Here Thy praises I'll begin;

Here I raise my Ebenezer [a stone of remembrance];
Here by Thy great help I've come;
And I hope, by Thy good pleasure,
Safely to arrive at home . . .

O to grace how great a debtor
Daily I'm constrained to be!
Let Thy goodness , like a fetter,
Bind my wandering heart to Thee.
Prone to wander, Lord, I feel it,
Prone to leave the God I love;
Here's my heart, O take and seal it,
Seal it for Thy courts above.[4]

I share this story to show that the road to finding hope (or any other virtue) and keeping it may be a rocky one. Pursuing any virtue is a process like most things. No one ever quite arrives. It's often a zigzag, three steps forward and two steps back. Each climb, though a struggle, is well worth it as we capture beautiful vistas and breathtaking panoramas; however, there are chasms and loose rocks that must be carefully traversed.

There is the success of making it to the top of the peak but realizing soon after there are many other peaks still ahead. It's that one day, after much climbing, that we hope to reach *our* Everest. Making it to the top may be the reward, but our lives (the journey), where all the work and development occurs, are what makes getting to the top worthwhile.

What Will Challenge Your Hope?

The polar opposites of hope are the conditions of fear and despair. It's been said by many that we often bring things to pass based upon the content of our thoughts. I believe that to be true. There is such a thing as the self-fulfilling prophecy, and if we are feeling hopeless, we're likely thinking similarly. These things may come about consciously or unconsciously.

Life is unpredictable. If we could see even a short distance ahead, we would still need hope; although we'd have more certainty. But then again that might be good, or it might be scary, depending on what we see in our future.

Losing hope is feeling as if your life's blood is draining out of you. It's that thin line that separates giving up or holding on.

Hope is hanging on when the odds seem stacked against you; hope is believing you'll beat cancer and get your life back; hope is believing your adult child will beat their drug addiction and find a better way to live; hope is believing you'll find real love, and be valued just for being you; hope is making that monthly payment with the desire to be out of debt; hope is seeing the world as a place of abundance and not a place of scarcity.

Hopelessness thrives in negativity, darkness, and disbelief. The following poem describes the challenges we all face—the human forces that wish to destroy hope:

"Listen to the mustn'ts, child.

Listen to the don'ts.

Listen to the shouldn'ts, the impossibles, the won'ts.

Listen to the never haves, then listen close to me . . . Anything can happen, child.

Anything can be."[5]

Don't let the grinches of pessimism rob you. Hold on to your own Christmas of hope. Hope, like the night before Christmas, has its own spirit, state of mind, and joyful feeling.

How to Make Hope Your Own

One of the most emotionally moving motion pictures in recent memory is *Hachi: A Dog's Tale* (2009) starring Richard Gere and Joan Allen. It's based on the true story of the love and devotion between a man and a dog.

In the movie, music professor Parker Wilson, played by Gere, encounters a lost puppy which had just arrived in freight from Japan. When the crate breaks open at the train station and with evening approaching and no one to claim him, Wilson takes the puppy home. The following day he tries to find its rightful owner but is unsuccessful.

As time passes, Wilson and the puppy, who he names Hachi, develop a very close bond. Hachi wants to spend every waking moment with his newfound friend.

One morning, Wilson leaves for work and finds Hachi following him to the train station, causing him to miss the train. When Wilson returns the following day, there is Hachi waiting faithfully at the depot. This pattern continues—day after day like clockwork.

One afternoon while at work, Wilson suffers an unexpected brain hemorrhage and dies. Hachi as usual waits loyally at his post at the train station. The hours pass, but he faithfully waits, *hopefully* expecting his master to appear. The weeks pass, and still he waits—with *hope*.

Wilson's family finds him at the station and do their best to take him home. But it doesn't work. Hachi returns to the station each day and vigilantly waits. When night falls, he sleeps in the rail yard. The hot dog seller grows to love Hachi and provides him with food and water each day.

Hachi continues sitting at his usual spot, day after day, month after month. The seasons come and go; still he remains steadfast, forever waiting, as months turn to years.

On the tenth anniversary of Wilson's death, his widow returns to the small township to visit her late husband's grave. She is stunned to come across a now very elderly Hachi, still waiting in place. Overcome with grief, she sits and waits with Hachi for that anticipated next train.

Hachi, ever faithful, and always hopeful, continues waiting until that final day when he is seen laying down in the snow.

Hope serves Hachi to the end, comforted by a dog's grandest vision. In it, Wilson suddenly appears—his best friend, and lovingly beckons him home!

There are many lessons and virtues found in this story (i.e., love, patience, loyalty, *hope*). When I see this movie, I see the everlasting *hope*, *both* in Hachi and among all people, who yearn to be reunited with those that they love—that's some kind of hope.

"There is no medicine like hope, no incentive so great, and no tonic so powerful as [an] expectation of something tomorrow."[6]

With any important trait that we seek, we can first begin by reading and studying all that is known about the trait. Why do we want this one particular virtue? How will it help or serve me in life? Who in my life has made an impact on me by incorporating hope into their heart and soul?

Benjamin Franklin was one of the great minds of the eighteenth century. He had a natural curiosity for life and made important contributions in the areas of science, music, literature and politics. (He just happens to be one of our greatest statesman.) He was always looking for ways to learn and improve. Very early in his life he sought to attain the goal of moral perfection. "I wish'd to live without committing any fault at any time. I would conquer all that either natural inclination, customs, or company might lead me into."[7]

Franklin created a method for self-improvement; each day, he monitored thirteen virtues by making a simple tabulation within in a small book that he carried around with him. He would place a dot next to each virtue that he had violated that day. His goal was to eventually minimize or eliminate the dots, ultimately signifying he was becoming more virtuous.

"Tho' I never arrived at the perfection I had been so ambitious of obtaining, but fell far short of it, yet I was, by the endeavor, a better and happier man than I otherwise should have been if I had not attempted it."[8]

If having more hope had been one of Franklin's sought for virtues, he might have purposely expressed more *hopeful,* encouraging words to others or taught himself to think more *hopeful* thoughts when faced with difficult situations.

Journaling about your life experiences is one way to script or promote positive thinking, which is another form of *hope.* As you write about what is happening around you, such as the COVID-19 pandemic, you can write how you see glimmers of *hope.* You can record the positive deeds being done by others and how you're getting through each day. This provides a further sense of *hope* for yourself and others.

Visualizing *hope* is its own paradigm and creates a brighter lens from which to see your way through.

I believe *hope,* like many of the other virtues, will likely manifest itself in our health. We know that those who are anxious and depressed suffer more emotionally and physically. Mental health professionals believe that stress plays a role in upwards of ninety percent of all physical health complaints.

There may be other factors involved in the struggle to find *hope.* Addressing these issues can make life better. For instance, those who feel unloved will find the world a more difficult place. If you're going through a difficult change or loss in your life, it may feel permanent, but it usually isn't. Try to remember when you have felt loved unconditionally by another and how it made your world a safer, happier place. Know that this kind of love and happiness is possible again. This is hope!

Avoid social isolation. This can add to a sense of despair. Seek for occasions to make contact with a friend to increase socialization. Try to meet for lunch, plan a walk, or to see a movie together; if not, phone a friend or loved one. These things can go a long way toward easing loneliness and the sense of disconnectedness. Encouraging yourself toward meaningful contact helps you lean toward hope, and increases a sense of *hopefulness.*

Create something to get excited about, something to look forward to. Perhaps a small vacation or meeting up with friends you haven't seen in a long time. When we have something fun planned in our near future, it draws us forward, and we generally become more *hopeful.*

Would finding something that deepens your purpose make a difference? It does for most. When you know the reason for your existence and can make a difference in others' lives, the meaning of life elevates to new heights. As this happens, it's much easier to get up and get going each day! This increases optimism and *hope.*

Many find that a connection to God or a higher power also lifts them. Sensing His presence helps many feel loved and that they belong. Believing you came from a place of love, and that that love is sustaining you, is empowering. When you come to an understanding of your true identity or real self, this will breed *hope.* Many believe this occurs after an experience with God or the Divine. It's reassuring to know you are loved and known by Him.

We all have trials and challenges in this life. Many of these difficulties seem unfair regardless of when they occur. We need hope to navigate the troubled waters that surely will come.

There is a most interesting story that without hope of the strongest kind would have likely ended in tragedy. It's about the perilous adventures of Steven Callahan. He was in a sailboat on his way across the Atlantic when the boat hit something, which immediately led to its sinking. In a short amount of time, he was miraculously able to inflate a raft that gave him a second chance. There he was, all alone, distanced from all the shipping lanes. Despite his ominous condition, he found ways to catch fish. He fixed himself a solar still, so he could turn the sea into drinkable water. Though these things helped, he remained horribly dehydrated and famished Hours turned to days and days into weeks. He wondered how he could keep on trying when all seemed lost.

"I knew I was totally alone . . . had a lot of time to think, and I regretted every mistake I'd ever made— was divorced, and felt I had failed at human relations generally, at business and now even at sailing. I desperately wanted to get through it so I could make a better job of my life."[9]

Desperation was setting in and personal suffering increasing. He was devastated when he realized the raft he was on was punctured. He made repeated attempts to repair it but was unsuccessful. It still leaked. He wondered what was next. Now, completely overwhelmed, he felt like giving up.

He said he felt like my body and mind were shutting down, remembering that he had no more to give. But he also sensed that,

"It was as if I could feel all the people who had ever been lost at sea— round me."[10]

In spite of these extreme circumstances, he did something with his mind. His thoughts helped him find the courage to keep going, to keep trying. History tells us that most survivors do something with their minds to help them find a way to carry on. Callahan wrote, "I told myself I can handle it. Compared to what others have been through, I'm fortunate. I told myself these things over and over again, building up a sense of fortitude [belief and strength]."[11]

The words he told himself proved to be powerful and likely saved him. After seventy-six days afloat (the longest anyone has survived a shipwreck—alone on a raft) three fishermen found him alive.

An important part of not giving up is to try to see your situation differently from where you are in the present moment. Think of the circumstances of others that have been much more desperate. Your situation could be worse. You are fortunate, blessed, and alive. There are lessons to learn, and the sun will shine again. There is something I can learn from this experience. There is still a plan for my life.

"What doesn't kill me makes me stronger."[12]

Sometimes our problems do seem insurmountable. When we are discouraged and feel like giving up, when all we see are roadblocks ahead, we can do what Steven Callahan did. Hold on, somehow, someway, and find those words that can literally change your life; I can get through this; this too will pass; I will survive.

Has there ever been a time you felt hopeless?

What were the circumstances?

Why was it hard to see light at the end of the tunnel?

What did you do (even if others assisted you) to become hopeful, to find the promise of a better day?

Encouragement can help each one of us and goes a long way toward finding hope. We can encourage ourselves, be encouraged by family and friends, and find hope in the stories of those who overcame difficult circumstances. Find and read some interesting biographies. There are few successful people, if any at all, who have not been "on the brink" at some time or another. The scriptures offer fascinating stories of those who defied all odds when all seemed hopeless.

When I was a young adult, I was at an evening church service where a gentleman came to speak to a rather large group. He was a leader over many congregations and was assigned to our specific geographical area. He had come to offer encouragement, support, and guidance to the members of the congregation. I'd heard him speak previously, but that night he was particularly honest and forthcoming. He obviously felt inspired, realizing there were those present who were struggling with despair or hopelessness.

All of us at any given time are concerned, worried, maybe even despairing over something difficult in our lives.

He went on to share that some years ago when he was much younger, he was married and running a small business. That business suffered some serious reversals, and he was about to lose everything. He became very discouraged and found himself standing at the banks of a large river in the winter. He was about to jump in to make it all go away. But the still small voice inside wouldn't let him—he felt and found a glimmer of hope. He returned to his car and drove home and in so doing, returned to his life. With added hope, he now squarely faced the challenges before him. He survived the ordeal and eventually found a new business where he became very successful. And may I add, he became even more respected as a spiritual leader in the region.

What are the Fruits of Hope?

How do you generate hope? It begins in a variety of ways.

It's often kindled through conversing with another, by reading and pondering, or receiving encouraging words. It comes as we draw on inspiration from someone or something. Hope rests in our minds and takes seed in our hearts. It comes from something you want in your life, perhaps what you really need.

Hope encourages patience, produces light, expands the feeling of encouragement. It "makes the present moment less difficult to bear" (Thich Nhat Hanh).

It allows us to hold on, to press on, when there is no certainty that deliverance will come.

Hope is patience with the lamp lit (Tertulian).

Chapter 2

Faith

"Don't you quit. You keep walking. You keep trying. There is help and happiness ahead. Some blessings come soon, some come late, and some don't come until heaven; but for those who embrace the gospel of Jesus Christ, they come. It will be all right in the end. Trust God and believe in good things to come."
—Jeffrey R. Holland

What Is Faith?

We've just spent considerable time looking at the importance of hope. Hope has been described as an expectation or desire for a certain thing to happen. So, what then is faith? How does it differ from hope? Though these two virtues are related, they are not the same.

"Hope means something we hold onto; faith is conviction and commitment, a reliance on God; Hope is the soil in which we exercise faith."[1]

According to the Oxford definition, faith is the complete trust or confidence one places in someone or something. Often, but not always, faith is associated with God or one's belief in a higher power.

Faith is a belief that takes us further down the road when the naysayers are naysaying, or when others might be giving up. It's a conviction that provides life-saving energy and a quiet confidence. When we exercise faith, it is stronger and more robust than hope. Real faith usually involves some type of action on our part. It's been said that faith without action is not enough. Strong or meaningful faith will usually impel a person to do something more than hoping and praying for some desired outcome. Prayer, though vitally important and a form of action, will often be followed with meaningful activity.

If you want a job, you'll likely need to make some phone calls and schedule some interviews. Think of a woman who wants to become a physician. She can have all the faith and confidence in her intelligence, GPA, and the score she received on the medical admissions test (MAT). However, she'll still need to travel for face-to-face interviews in order to gain acceptance to a medical school. She will need to attend and complete medical school, do a residency, and pass her board exams. All these involve study and the application of knowledge and skills (action)—an important part of the activating power of faith. One spiritual leader of millions recently said regarding faith,

"The Lord loves effort, because effort brings reward that cannot come without it."[2]

The scriptures teach similarly "*What doth it profit, my brethren, though a man say he hath faith, and have not works? Can faith save him?* If a brother or sister be naked, and destitute of daily food, and one of you say unto them, Depart in peace, be ye warmed and filled; notwithstanding ye give them not those things which are needful to the body; what doth it profit? Even so faith, if it hath not works, is dead, being alone."[3]

Faith principles are every bit as applicable in our temporal pursuits. Fixing the mind upon a goal, then performing the necessary steps to get there, will usually take one to its realization.

Faith in the Goal and in the Self

In my previous book *Secrets for Hope and Healing* I gave a clear example of how one can operationalize an important goal. When a person really wants to achieve something, they need to write the goal down. Making the goal more sensory will enliven and deepen it in both the conscious and unconscious mind. When you can see, hear, touch, taste, and smell (so to speak) the goal, you know it's becoming tangible and likely attainable. When you can also "feel" that it's coming about, it becomes another important dimension. Making the goal reachable will happen as you create a vision board. This vision board is a poster or a designated place on a wall where you'll place pictures, words, or statements that flesh out your goal in greater detail. Spending a few minutes each day visualizing the goal(s) on the vision board will enhance and intensify what you seek. There is much written on the internet on how to construct a vision board; go there if you need more assistance. A vision board is like throwing gasoline on an idea, more specifically your idea. Writing a book was one of my goals. It started as an idea, then fleshed out through much effort and ultimately brought to fruition. This is the process of bringing about the things you want to do. I know that things would not have happened for me without the vision board. I can tell you I have used it and it works.

The power of visualized goals and beliefs is dynamic.

The impact of the mind on our health is unmistakable, and that influence is of increasing interest. Studies over the last few decades are making this clearer:

> Mind/body medicine should remind us of the precious nature of our minds . . . automatic negative thoughts, bad moods and compulsive worrying eventually take up physical residence in our bodies . . . living well, exercising and eating appropriately, seeing doctors when you need to but not over-relying on the medical system—these are all proven buffers against disease and illness . . . Believe in something good. Even though we do not necessarily need all the pills and procedures, these medicinal symbols retain an aura of effectiveness and often appease our desire for action . . . [We ought] to wean ourselves from excessive spending on unnecessary therapies, [but we seem to] need some catalysts for belief, even if belief is really the healer . . . So remember the vigor from the time you felt healthiest in your life . . . Believe in something good if you can. Or even better, believe in something better than anything you can fathom. Because for us mortals, this is very profound medicine.[4]

Faith in Others

As the definition of faith implies, having trust and confidence in another is important. There are, of course, degrees of faith or trust. I have met several people recently who feel they have lost the ability to trust other humans. We all know these people; they invest in animals, sometimes a lot of them, in different varieties. Cats and dogs, rabbits and snakes, exotic fish and birds. I even knew of a ferret that lived in the person's sofa. The sky is the limit when it comes to making animals your friends.

As human beings, we let each other down. We violate trust, betray confidences, and fail in being reliable. Our transgressions may even be bigger than these things when there is serious abuse or neglect. However, no one is perfect, and we all need to forgive and be forgiven. We all fall short and need a little grace. I'm certainly not saying that someone should risk continual hurt and damage to their mind, body, or spirit. There's a time when enough is enough.

Having faith in another person allows us to make a connection; to not feel alone or isolated; to feel loved or cared for, and to be a part of something more than ourselves, which we all seem to need. Having faith is relying on and trusting one another. It's letting that person into our world in the deepest sense possible, letting them see not only the good but perhaps the worst parts of us. That may be incredibly difficult, but it is possible to do. For a relationship to be truly viable, faith and trust are necessary, whether it be romantic, marital, friendship, therapeutic, or even business oriented.

Faith in another person is a belief and a trust that you extend to them. You believe they will bless your life in some way. It can be provisional at first and then may deepen over time. If there's a violation, it can be addressed and worked through.

The best friendships have these qualities; therefore, one can have a true and abiding faith in another person regardless of their imperfections.

Working in the health profession has allowed me to see the influence caregivers can have with patients. When a patient has faith in their physician or caregiver, it can make a difference in their healing and health outcomes. The power of placebo, the effect that comes from a person's expectations, is a part of that.

Faith in God

"To one who has faith, no explanation is necessary. To one without faith, no explanation is possible."[5]

Herbert Benson, famed cardiologist at Harvard and a major contributor to the wellness movement, believed "that religious faith was more powerful than affirmative beliefs."[6]

Faith in a Supreme Being is having trust that He is near.

My first memories of the word faith involved the idea of faith in God or a higher power. It was probably during a children's Sunday School class that I learned this. I was taught then, and still believe to this day, that we have a Heavenly Father that knows and loves us and has an absolute interest in our lives. Just as our earthly parents (or the mentors who became our surrogate parents) love us and are concerned about our welfare; imagine a Father in Heaven, the creator of all things including our spirit which is housed in our body, and of His vast love and concern for us.

Because He is our Father and has all power, He has the motivation and capacity to guide and influence us. He has and is perfect love, and along with the design of mortality, will from time to time intervene in our lives. Much of the time he will not interfere with our choices so we may learn from them. His involvement in both the critical and noncritical events of our life remains somewhat of a mystery while we're here on earth.

Those who believe—will receive manifestations, the tender mercies bestowed upon us through the Holy Ghost. The Holy Ghost is a spirit personage, a member of the Godhead sent to enlighten and inspire us with truth of any kind. These witnesses may be experienced through dreams or aha moments or from people who arrive right on time to help us in our want and need or through miracles, etc. The scriptures tell us that

"Signs will follow (be given to) those who believe."[7]

It takes faith to see His hand in our lives, but He is present if we are "still," and observe. There are angels (resurrected beings and those not yet born) that come from the other side to help us. They usually remain unseen—but not always. I have heard too many stories from completely sane people regarding various forms of divine intervention. It's a demonstration of His love and interest in our lives.

There was a wonderful video series produced on the ministry of Christ, and released this past year called The *Chosen*. There have been so many productions made about Christ, one can only wonder what more can be said or done. This series is very moving, and the script and characters seem most authentic. With the event of COVID-19, the director Dallas Jenkins, was unable to secure a time and place to film Season 2. They looked everywhere in the world—nothing was working out.

Dallas fervently prayed and asked others interested in the project to join him in finding an answer to their dilemma. He reported soon thereafter that doors began to fly open, and what had been a "no" to the perfect site (a man-made replica of the city of Jerusalem in Utah) turned into a "yes." He was most grateful and gave praises to the Father. He believes what he experienced was a miracle delivered because of the faith and prayers of the group.[8]

He referenced the words of a Christian song that captured his joy when the solution was found:

'Cause You make mountains move, You make giants fall,
And you use songs of praise to shake prison walls;
And I will speak to my fear, I will preach to my doubt
That You were faithful then, You'll be faithful now.[9]

This story and song are emblematic of how true believers think and feel and how the power of God can influence the events of our lives.

What will Challenge Our Faith ?

Exercising faith is not an exercise that's undertaken like a scientific experiment. It's not about replicated studies, validity, or data-driven research.

"Faith is not to have a perfect knowledge of things."[10]

It's about believing and relying on a power that is not seen but that is real.

According to research done at the University of Toronto, most Americans believe God is concerned with their personal well-being and is directly involved in their personal affairs. The study found that 82 percent of Americans say they depend on God for help and guidance in making decisions. Interestingly, it was found that even the well-educated and those with higher incomes (as well as those very involved in religious rituals), share similar levels of beliefs about divine intervention as their less educated and less financially well-off peers.[11]

What this means is that it isn't just the poor or economically challenged that "cling to guns and religion," as one politician put it but that people of all races and groups, and walks of life still possess strong faith.[12]

Most people won't talk about their spiritual experiences due to their concern that others will think they are crazy. If you're sincere and gain their trust and they are so inclined, many will share their stories with you.

I remember visiting a woman in her 80s in the rehab unit of the hospital. For this story, I'll call her Ellen. We got to talking and she felt inspired to share her story. It must have been weighing on her mind, as I think now in retrospect. She was wondering if her work here on earth was done. She explained that her husband had passed away a few years earlier, and then she too became ill and found herself on death's door. She was not expected to live. During the night she had a dream. Her husband told her that it wasn't her time and that she still had a work to do. She survived the night and returned to health. Not many months later, her son divorced, and neither he nor the child's mother was capable of raising their teenage daughter. Ellen explained that she didn't want the responsibility—but felt compelled to take the granddaughter in. In spite of her advanced age, she felt she'd succeeded in raising her. Now, some years later, the girl was nearing the completion of her senior year of high school. As Ellen finished the story, she seemed to question if her work was finished, and if it was time for her to "go home."

More recently I was visiting with another woman hospitalized with chest pain. She was also of similar age. I'll refer to her as Barbara. She reported that she was lonely and would like to have another relationship. I was a bit surprised of her desires at this advanced age, forgetting that a loving relationship is an eternal quest for most people, most of the time. After some informal chitchat, she recounted that she'd been married several times, though never blessed with children of her own. She wanted to know if I was Christian and a "believer." I told her that I was. She proceeded to disclose several spiritual experiences to me. She related that in a two-month stretch just a few years previous, she witnessed the visits of three spirit beings in her home. Each lasted only a few seconds and none of the spirits communicated out loud. The first was the figure of a being she did not recognize; the second was a visit from her deceased first husband, someone she'd spent thirty-four years with and whom she still loved. Finally, she saw her mother who looked at her directly but did not speak a word. When I asked why she thought these things had happened, she replied, "I think it was to give me comfort, that those we knew and loved in life are closer than we think; that they care about us and are mindful of our lives."

Faith is a big part of many people's lives. Once others know they will not be mocked, their stories are told unabashedly. Spirit-filled stories of faith provide strength and reassurance for us during the struggles and challenges we face in life.

For many, faith is an inherent thing. It has its own logic even if it can't be proven; it's familiar though not visibly seen. Paul said in Romans, "How then shall they call on him in whom they have not believed? And how shall they believe in him of whom they have not heard?"[13]

The seeds of faith and beliefs largely come about because someone (usually a parent or mentor) explained who God is and how faith works. Now having the beginnings of faith, many go on to have spiritual experiences of their own—about things that cannot be explained in any other way.

How Do We Increase Our Faith?

Let me tell you a story—one of the best ways we learn. Think of your own faith, and liken it to a seed—a farmer's seed. Now we all know that seeds were made to grow; to grow into something bigger and something very useful. Imagine that seed as a grain of wheat. If the seed is true, if it's healthy and whole, its capacity is extraordinary.

Faith is like a seed. It may be rather small, even dormant, but within it lies the great potential to grow and flourish and ultimately feed one's soul. Like a seed that requires fertile ground, faith must also be planted in the fertile places of our minds and hearts. For faith to take root, some belief is required. It needn't be strong or sure at first, it just needs a place to be planted-just as one might exercise a particle of faith or belief in something.

If the seed receives water, light, and warmth, it will germinate or swell from within. It's beginning to grow. If we receive truth in any form and do not resist or cast it out, we too may begin to feel the "swelling motions" within ourselves. We may describe the faith experience as one of enlightenment, of increased understanding. Our faith is taking root and growing (Alma 32:28).

Just as the seed "swelleth and sprouteth and beginneth to grow," so can our faith. As the seed strengthens, so does our faith; and we conclude that the seed is good, for it bringeth forth its own likeness (Alma 32:30).

As the seed grows and expands and finally breaks through the darkness of the soil, so too will our minds break free, towards additional light and truth. Just like the seed and the mind, each begin to fill the measure of their creation.

As the seed grows, we begin to realize that we must "nourish it with great care so that it may get root and grow up" and produce fruit. If we neglect the plant or our faith, either can lose their root, and "when the heat cometh and scorcheth it," it will wither away (Alma 32:37–38).

If we nourish truth with an eye of faith, "with diligence and patience, looking forward to the fruit, it will take root and be a living thing that springs up everlastingly." At harvest time, we'll be able to "pluck the fruit." It will be most precious, sweet, white, and pure; we "shall feast upon this fruit even until we are filled" (Alma 32:42).

This is an allegory of faith, and it describes how faith can be acquired and grow to a level of knowing rather than only believing.

What Are Its Fruits?

The scriptures are replete with this phrase: "Signs will follow those who believe in me!" Signs may be miracles, warnings, evidences of God's reality, demonstrations of His love and power. Many have witnessed themselves or others being healed through prayer and faith.

Not uncommon, is the experience through our faith, of receiving inspiration and revelation to life's challenges and questions. This inspiration may come through visions or dreams but more frequently comes through impressions in the mind and feelings in the heart. Many report that it comes in the moments when the mind is fresh and undisturbed by the stresses of the day. For many, it is in the stillness of the morning or night and away from distraction. Many report that during an early-morning shower, walk, or in the stillness (meditation), that these inspirations come.

I believe that intelligence flows or is more plentiful when we're asking in faith for truth or wisdom, especially in our effort to bless others or make the world a better place.

I was riding my bike in the country as I do several days of the week. It was an early-spring morning early in the pandemic, one of those days when the air was fresh, the sky was blue, and everything was near perfect. It was rather quiet, and I was virtually alone . . . it's times like this that I get inspiration. It usually just starts with ideas flowing through my mind. This book started in that same fashion. I knew it was inspiration by the quality of the ideas and feelings I received (see Pratt's definition in the chapter on Wisdom). I especially try to pay attention when I feel it's coming from a higher source.

I believe you know what I am talking about. The key is to pay attention. It really is pure energy flowing in. If you have not done so already, think about when you are most apt to receive this kind of inspiration. Stop and take notice next time; write it down in a journal. Figure out what you're receiving and why it's coming, and move forward with it. Is it part of what you desire, something you've been pursuing? Is the information in your current wheelhouse or taking you in a new direction? I believe it is usually something important, and it is what He wants you to pay attention to. If it's real and from Him, honor it and Him, and He will give you more.

I believe all of this is part of the continuum of faith!

Chapter 3

Wisdom

"By three methods we may learn wisdom: First, by reflection, which is noblest; Second, by imitation, which is easiest; and third by experience, which is the bitterest." —Confucius

What Is Wisdom?

How many of you think of yourselves as wise? My first impressions of the wise are of wizards, prophets, or really old people with great knowledge. The wise generally have great skill in analyzing things, and in human relations. I believe many of us think wisdom is not easily attainable and is something almost other-worldly.

Wisdom has been defined as having knowledge of what is true and right. It is possessing the ability to make just judgments. It's about having discernment, insight, and perceptiveness.

"The unexamined life is not worth living."[1]

I don't know about you, but most of the time I don't feel so wise. In fact, I think there are few people I would describe in a manner as wise. There are many that fit the bill of being educated, knowledgeable, even brilliant. But wise, that is a different category altogether.

Though loads of information can be disseminated by knowledgeable people, this doesn't necessarily make them wise. We go to the internet for so much, and its accuracy can be suspect. There is deception everywhere. Everyone has a pitch and a purpose in what they propagate. Having access to information is not enough. Applying knowledge in a meaningful way, leads to wisdom and truth.

I think I reserve the label of wise to those who have lived a full, long life, say at least seventy-five years. They've probably endured significant changes in our world, such as wars, depressions and recessions, and other upheavals found in society. They will have been married (or had a serious committed love relationship), and preferably have had children. They will have experienced their own personal pain from health, wealth, and relationship challenges. They will have faced rejection, grief, loneliness; experienced anger, love, hope, joy, and happiness.

For me, they have been spiritual and or religious, and if neither, have spent some serious time contemplating the meaning of life. They'll have had "questions" for and/or serious conversations with the Almighty. They will have experienced inspiration, revelation, or epiphanies (those aha moments) where the universe (God) has spoken to them in some important way. Wise people see and hear things and have found the meaning and purpose of life, both the personal and the universal. They likely possess many of the virtues found in this book. They have insight and they "get it."

Albert Einstein once said, "Wisdom is not a product of schooling but of the lifelong attempt to acquire it."[2]

Of course, all these things aren't necessarily required; they're just part of my list. But it makes a big difference when a person has learned from the gamut of life's experiences and acquired and filtered all sorts of knowledge from living. The following quote bears this out: "Many people mistake knowledge for wisdom . . . knowledge is the accumulation of facts and information. Wisdom is the synthesis of knowledge and experiences into insights that deepen one's understanding of relationships and the meaning of life. In other words, knowledge is a tool, and wisdom is the craft in which the tool is used."[3]

Thus, it seems-wisdom is the obtaining and the grooming of virtues through our life experiences. They come in a variety of ways, but I think there are chiefly two. The first is the way Benjamin Franklin pursued the process. He identified what he desired and then systematically and consciously went about the task. He kept a record on how he was doing and measured his progress. The SMART goal folks would have liked his approach. The second way is stumbling into those virtues through the school of hard knocks. By living life and doing our best, we learn, grow, and increase in wisdom. The first method may come about sooner, as it's a pursuit with an organized effort.

I turn to scripture, which for me states that wisdom is God's gift to humans who seek to fashion their life to become more like His. Though perfection isn't possible in this life, Jesus wants us to become all that we can be and gave us what seemed to be the impossible task when He said, "Be ye therefore perfect even as your Father which is in heaven is perfect."[4]

We are in an apprenticeship, and it's only through time and experience that we grow and develop, should we want to be like Them. It is choosing to follow in His footsteps and live and abide by His teachings. Modern scripture reveals how this can occur: "I will give unto the children of men line upon line, precept upon precept, here a little and there a little; and blessed are those who hearken unto my precepts, and lend an ear unto my counsel, for they shall learn wisdom; for unto him the receiveth I will give more."[5]

In other words, we learn gradually, often through trial and error; we will not "get it" all at first. We gain insight and incorporate the meaning of life's lessons day by day. This teaching suggests wisdom is God's gift for following Him.

From additional scripture, we are told to seek the gift of wisdom: "Wisdom is the principal thing; therefore get wisdom: and with all thy getting get understanding," (Proverbs 4:7).

"For wisdom is better than rubies; and all the things that may be desired are not to be compared to it"(Proverbs 8:11).

"All saints who remember to keep [the law of health and] the commandments . . . shall find wisdom and great treasures of knowledge, even hidden treasures"(Doctrine & Covenants 89:18–19).

"Wisdom is better than strength" (Ecclesiastes 9:16).

"Let him that is ignorant learn wisdom by humbling himself and calling upon the Lord his God, that his eyes may be opened that he may see, and his ears opened that he may hear"(Doctrine and Covenants 136:32).

When you possess any gift, think of how you can help, support, and inspire others. Think how a person of faith helps one who is downtrodden and hopeless; how a compassionate person teaches others to love; how forgiveness sets both parties free.

In the words of the apostle Paul, "Brethren, whatsoever things are true, whatsoever things are honest, whatsoever things are just, whatsoever things are pure, whatsoever things are lovely, whatsoever things are of good report; if there be any virtue, and if there be any praise, think on these things" (Philippians 4:8).

A challenging but worthwhile standard.

King Solomon, the son of David of Old Testament times, was only about fifteen years old when he ascended the throne. Feeling overwhelmed by his duties, God appeared to him in a dream and asked how He might help him. The following passage describes what happened:

And Solomon loved the Lord, walking in the statutes of David his father: [and] he sacrificed . . . a thousand burnt offerings . . . upon [the] altar. In Gibeon the Lord appeared to Solomon in a dream by night: and God said, *Ask what I shall give thee . . .*

I am but a little child: I know not how to go out or come in [how to govern]. And thy servant is in the midst of thy people . . . a great people, that cannot be numbered nor counted for multitude. *Give therefore thy servant an understanding heart to judge thy people, that I may discern between good and bad: for who is able to judge this thy so great a people?*

And the speech pleased the Lord, that Solomon had asked this thing. And God said unto him, Because thou hast asked [for] this thing, and hast not asked for thyself [a] long life; neither hast asked riches for thyself, nor hast asked [for] the life of thine enemies; but hast asked for thyself understanding to discern judgment; *Behold, I have done according to thy words:* lo, I have given thee a wise and an understanding heart; so that there was none like thee before thee, neither after thee shall any arise like unto thee. And I have also given thee that which thou hast not asked, both riches, and honour: so that there shall not be any among the kings like unto thee all thy days. And if thou wilt walk in my ways, to keep my statutes and my commandments . . . then I will lengthen thy days.

> And Solomon awoke . . . And all Israel heard of [his] judge-
> ment . . . and they feared the king: for they saw that the wisdom
> of God was in him.[6]

One way that wisdom comes about is through the development of our minds by increasing our intelligence. This is accomplished through the processing of information that we hope is useful to us now and in the future. Wisdom, or percolated knowledge (that which has been filtered), actually comes to us in three basic ways: through our minds, our emotions, and our spirit. Though we are one being or organism, we have different channels for learning; thus, we can develop cognitive intelligence (IQ), emotional intelligence (EI), and spiritual intelligence (SQ).

The word *intelligence* is derived from the Latin word *intelligentia* or *intelligere*, meaning to comprehend or perceive. In the middle ages this word was a scholarly term for understanding. Interestingly, intelligence was strongly linked to the metaphysical and cosmological theories of learning. For most of the last century, the focus has been to define intelligence as pertaining to one's cognitive or mental capacities.

In trying to come up with an accurate definition for intelligence (IQ), a number of scientists in the mid-1990s defined it as "a very general mental capability that, among other things, involves the ability to reason, plan, solve problems, think abstractly, comprehend complex ideas, learn quickly and learn from experience. It is not merely book learning, a narrow academic skill, or test-taking smarts. Rather, it reflects a broader and deeper capability for comprehending our surroundings—'catching on,' 'making sense' of things, or 'figuring out' what to do."[7]

One year later in 1995, the American Psychological Association described intelligence this way:

> Individuals differ from one another in their ability to understand
> complex ideas, to adapt effectively to the environment, to learn
> from experience, to engage in various forms of reasoning, to over-
> come obstacles [through] thought. Although these individual
> differences can be substantial, they are never entirely consistent:
> a given person's intellectual performance will vary on different

occasions, in different domains, as judged by different criteria. The APA went on to conclude that no such conceptualization of intelligence can answer all the important questions, nor can any body or group find universal agreement as to its meaning.[8]

In other words, intelligence is difficult to define and in any consistent way.

Emotional intelligence is another type of knowledge, another way of knowing the world. In simple terms, it's the ability to recognize, understand, and manage our emotions. It also includes recognizing, understanding, and influencing the emotions of others. The term emotional intelligence, referred to as El, was first coined by researchers Peter Salavoy and John Mayer, then popularized by Dan Goleman. According to Goleman, EI consists of five areas:

1. Self-awareness: the capacity to know one's emotions, assets and deficits, motives, goals and desires, and their effects on others.

2. Self-regulation: the ability to manage or redirect difficult emotions and adjust to changing situations.

3. Social skill: the ability to develop and manage relationships with others.

4. Empathy: sensing and considering other's feelings as one makes decisions.

5. Motivation: an awareness of what drives or motivates us.[9]

Most of us appreciate the gifts of smart people, but we also realize that brilliance is not enough to successfully navigate life. Most of us would agree that bright people with good social skills are the ones who are most successful. These are the ones we want to lead us, the ones we want to be around.

When we have emotional intelligence, we more readily recognize the dissonance in people and situations and can respond in ways that show empathy. EI can help us to work through conflicts and other challenges in all kinds of relationships.

Spirituality, or spiritual intelligence (SI),is another important way to gain knowledge. It has been defined as a source of ultimate concern for humans, reflecting a perceived connectedness to the transcendental, and the highest levels of cognitive, moral, emotional, and interpersonal development.[10]

"Being spiritually intelligent is a reflection of how deep an individual's capacity is in understanding existential questions . . . in its truest form, spirituality takes place in the mind and heart."[11]

SI has been described by Dr. Mark Atkinson as "harnessing the power [that provides the key] to purity, prosperity and happiness, and to [ultimately] creating paradise on earth."[12]

I like best, the definition offered by Parley P. Pratt when he described spirituality as one who is under the influence, or that has an abundance of the Holy Spirit. He said that this power:

> . . . quickens all the intellectual faculties, increases, enlarges, expands, and purifies all the natural passions and affections, and adapts them, by the gift of wisdom, to their lawful use. It inspires, develops, cultivates, and matures all the fine-toned sympathies, joys, tastes, kindred feelings, and affections of our nature. It inspires virtue, kindness, goodness, tenderness, gentleness, and charity. It develops beauty of person, form, and features. It tends to health, vigor, animation, and social feeling. It invigorates all the faculties of the physical and intellectual man. It strengthens and gives tone to the nerves. In short, it is, as it were, marrow to the bone, joy to the heart, light to the eyes, music to the ears, and life to the whole being.[13]

This a spiritual person, one who has developed their spiritual IQ.

What Will Challenge Authentic Wisdom?

Wisdom is not a showy thing, rather it's the humble understanding of life gained from trial and error through life's ups and downs. It has been acquired through blood, sweat, and tears, for that is the price of experience.

Advanced degrees or a prestigious education will make one full of earthly knowledge but not necessarily wise. That is obtained by mental, emotional and spiritual intelligence. It comes to those with their feet on the ground, who see the connections and blessings of both the seen and unseen world. An ancient wiseman said,

> O the vainness, and the frailties, and the foolishness of men! When they are learned they think they are wise, and they hearken not unto the counsel of God, for they set it aside, supposing they know of themselves, wherefore, their wisdom is foolishness and it profiteth them not . . . But to be *learned* is good if they hearken unto the counsels of God . . . And whoso knocketh, to him will he open; and the wise and the learned, and they that are rich, who are puffed up . . . he will not open up to them, [unless they] come down in the depths of humility.[14]

If we find our minds darkened, we will not have access to the best fruits. If we want something better, we must open ourselves up. Putting it in another way, if we listen to the still small voice by honoring and following it, we will be inspired to make the best decisions that will be a blessing to many.

When we honor and follow our conscience, which is the light and the wisdom He gives, we will be given more and more and more.

How to Generate Wisdom of Your Own

All the virtues one can have come as gifts from God. We possess some gifts naturally, though they likely will need some refinement. Those gifts that we need to develop will likely involve hard work.

Wisdom is the reward of the many gifts you harvest through your life. A fuller, deeper, richer life with many varied experiences leads to a certain level of wisdom as well.

We are commended to "seek earnestly the best gifts, always remembering for what they are given. For . . . they are given for the benefit of those who love me and keep my commandments and him that seeketh so to do; that all may be benefited that seek or that ask of me . . . all these gifts come from God, for the benefit of the children of God."[15]

If we ask for gifts for the purpose of helping and serving others, we will gain those gifts if it is His will; we are consequently blessed then with wisdom.

"And behold, I tell you these things that ye may learn wisdom; that ye may learn that when ye are in the service of your fellow beings ye are only in the service of your God."[16]

What Are the Fruits of Wisdom?

Wisdom is gaining knowledge and synthesizing it toward truth. I am Christian, a Latter-day Saint Christian. I love what I have and believe. To the truths I already have, such as those found in other philosophies and places, I add more. I've found that the contributions of Buddhism, such as mindfulness meditation, and teachings on happiness and suffering, also offer profound truth and further enrich my life.

We can plant the seeds of faith and truth from a variety of sources, watching to see if they bear fruit.

I was always told to "prove all things, hold fast [to] that which is good, [and that] only if you are unafraid of truth can you find it, [and in doing so, it will] lead to limitless opportunities."[17]

Wisdom is the joining of knowledge, life experiences, and discernment with a combined distillation coming from a heavenly source. James says: "But the wisdom that is from above is first pure, then peaceable, gentle, and easy to be intreated, full of mercy and good fruits, without partiality, and without hypocrisy. And the fruit of righteousness is sown in peace of them that make peace."[18]

Thus, the fruits of wisdom are peace and plenty—in all its forms.

The Virtues of Sacrifice

Humility, Repentance, Patience

Regrets or mistakes help us grow and should never define who we really are. Being "brought down" is an important part of our education, which can ultimately bring us back up again. The virtues of sacrifice help us see that change is possible and that we can become the best version of ourselves. Patience is power and will bring its own rewards.

Chapter 4

Humility

"I have been driven many times upon my knees by the overwhelming conviction that I had nowhere else to go. My own wisdom and that of all about me seemed insufficient for that day." —Abraham Lincoln

What Is Humility?

One of the biggest enemies to becoming better and in seeking personal improvement is pride. Being the opposite of humility, pride has also been described as the condition of being arrogant or boastful. "I am fine the way I am; why should I change?" or "My life is pretty good, because I've got mine!" Pride is a stumbling block, and some have suggested that it is the origin of all other vices and troubles.

J. M. Barrie has said, "Life is a long lesson in humility."[1]

Most of us are preoccupied with our own successes and accomplishments. The world would have us look for our fifteen minutes of fame, as expressed by Andy Warhol. Now, it's true more than ever, with YouTube, Instagram, TikTok, and other types of media self-promotion. Many have equated humility with weakness or inadequacy. Of course, that isn't true; it's just the new world order where showboating is a sign of power.

"We are all apprentices in a craft where no one becomes a master."[2]

We are all novices, and we should never think we are better than another person. I spoke to an older gentleman recently who was a patient in our hospital. He said that he was a D student in high school, and some thought he wouldn't amount to much. He was really good at business and numbers, and he found ways to continually pick up ground until he was a thriving, successful farmer. He had some really bad years like all farmers do. This helped him stay humble, knowing ultimately that what he had acquired was a blessing from God.

> The clearest way to identify humility is to see if the person is Christ-occupied or self-occupied. When somebody is arrogant, proud, and self-confident he is clearly self-occupied. At the other extreme, someone who is always fearful also has a problem with pride even if he appears to be very soft spoken and gentle. Instead of looking to Jesus, this person is self-conscious and constantly looking at himself. Both extremes are manifestations of pride. While one extreme manifests pride in terms of arrogance, the other extreme manifest pride in terms of self-consciousness. As long as a person is occupied with self, that is still pride. Humility then, is being Christ-occupied. This person knows that without the Lord, he cannot succeed, but with the Lord, all things are possible.[3]

People who are genuinely humble actually have strong characters. They have developed an awareness not to become occupied with the self. Their focus is on helping and serving others rather than what they can get from others. An authentic person knows they have value and is quick to recognize and acknowledge the value of others.

A humble person may be proficient with their own knowledge and skills, but are they equally proficient with people skills? With humility comes the receptiveness to others that is peaceful and steady. A humble person, though bright and insightful, will continue to listen to and keep learning from others. Being humble puts others at ease so that they feel comfortable and emotionally safe.

It seems there's a natural propensity for the world to divide into groups. One basic dichotomy is the "haves and have-nots." When we're in a state of pride, we focus on things. When we place too much value on things, we don't want to lose them. So, rather than share them, we withhold our material things and our talents; even worse, we make sure others have less than we do. This is referred to as a scarcity mentality. In it only some will have and control the resources.

"Pride must die in you, or nothing of heaven can live in you."
—Andrew Murray, *Humility: The Journey Toward Holiness*

"There is no room for God in him who is full of himself."[4]

It's amazing when a humble person with material things chooses to be generous or helpful. They look for others who can be assisted to regain their footing and move forward with their lives. Examples might include helping someone with a scholarship for education, securing funding to help a lower socioeconomic person start a small business or mentoring those coming out of prison to find meaningful work. These are examples of humble love "where a rising tide lifts all boats."[5]

There are many more of us who could engage in similar endeavors to lift the lives of others. When both the helper and the helped make contributions and become viable, our communities truly prosper.

What Will Challenge Our Desire for Humility?

Most of us consider pride to be a sin of those on the top, such as the rich and the learned, looking down on us. There is however, a far more common ailment among us—and that is pride from the bottom looking up. It is manifest in so many ways, such as fault-finding, gossiping, backbiting, and murmuring, living beyond our means, envying, coveting, withholding gratitude and praise that might lift another, and being unforgiving and jealous.[6]

It has been said that "things" tend to own us rather than the reverse. And that seems to be true. With things of material value comes prestige, position, and power. Few seem to be able to walk away or give them up, for they are intoxicating. In the words of C. S. Lewis: "Pride gets no pleasure out of something, only out of having more of it than the next man . . . It is the comparison that makes you proud: the pleasure of being above the rest. Once the element of competition is gone, pride has gone."[7]

"We have learned by sad experience that it is the nature and disposition of almost all men, as soon as they get a little authority, as they suppose, they will immediately begin to exercise *unrighteous* dominion."[8]

Many have written or alluded to the proverbial truth that "pride goeth before destruction, and an haughty spirit before a fall."[9]

Some have described a four-stage process that humans struggle with, almost always repeatedly. It's known as the Pride Cycle, and it occurs in society, as well as in our personal lives. It's not that we are destined to follow the cycle, it's just difficult to overcome it, by being continually humble and teachable thereby avoiding the entrapment of pride. The stages of the Pride Cycle are as follows:

1. Prosperity and confidence
2. Pride, over-confidence, and sin
3. Destruction, loss of confidence, and suffering
4. Humility and repentance

In *stage one* of **Prosperity,** we are doing well in our lives. We've likely sacrificed time and energy and worked really hard to make headway with our family or occupation, or both. We have tried to live by many of the virtues described herein. Think of faith, patience, self-mastery, fairness, among many others. Sustained effort and creativity are elements of success, and have likely played a role in helping us get to where we wanted to be. And now, finally, we are reaping the rewards—the fruits of our labors, the fruits of virtue.

Pride comes along in *stage two.* It's here where we've become maybe a little too sure of ourselves and our brilliance. We may become arrogant—inwardly or outwardly boastful. We think to ourselves, "I did that." It becomes easier to justify and rationalize things, even when they're not ethical. We become too focused on *our own things* and the *special person we've become.* With pride, we compare ourselves to others, usually with a belief of, "I'm better than so-and-so!" A prideful mind and heart can lead to dishonest actions (lying, stealing, cheating, etc.) or worse. Because of the law of justice and consequences, we're about to face the music.

In *stage three* of **Destruction,** things begin to implode. In the Bible, Hosea states that because of their hypocrisy, they "shall reap the whirlwind"

(Hosea 8:7). Matthew describes prideful people as "whitewashed tombs which indeed appear beautiful outwardly, but inside are full of dead men's bones and all uncleanness" (Matthew 23:27). It's here that we experience the pain of past actions. We may lose respect or standing, face fines or penalties, the withdrawal of love, experience family or marital distress.

"If pain doesn't lead to humility, you have wasted your suffering."[10]

The *fourth stage* of **Humility** brings the opportunity for relief from the pain and agony of destruction. We get another chance. If we choose to be meek and mild from our suffering, if we repent, we'll begin to feel hope once again. If we stop blaming others or the universe for what happened and begin to take responsibility, we may feel a type of cleansing; the refiner's fire at work in our souls. We can rebuild and will begin to prosper. Prosperity is not always about temporal wealth but may be an emotional or spiritual prosperity. We will, however, almost always have some kind of restoration, and enough!

"This is the cycle of pride. Our own personal Pride Cycle is the battle we have with ourselves. It's the result of our self-serving thoughts, feelings, and behavior. It ebbs and flows through our lives each time we become impressed with our looks, wealth, or achievements. We begin to think in our hearts that we are better than others. Of course, by being human, we will fall from the perch through the loss of material things, diminishments of age, poor judgment or decisions, and a host of other factors.

The antidote for pride is humility, gentleness, meekness, patience, long-suffering, and all the manifestations of love.

Humility is about having low self-preoccupation, not low self-esteem.[11]

If we were to follow the second great commandment in the law as taught by Jesus Christ "to love our neighbor as ourselves," would this not address and fix many of the world's ills? Love and humility, like the rest of the virtues, cannot be governed or forced into the hearts and minds of humans. Character grows as one consciously seeks virtue and nourishes it. Humility is latently present, planted in our hearts by the God of us all, if we'll listen to "the better angels of our nature."[12]

How Do We Foster Our Own Humility?

We tend to think of all the difficulties and challenges we'll have when we try to live in a humble way. It may be that the straight gate and narrow way is less traveled or familiar, but it's one that's sure.

> Humility is like a magnet that attracts favor, attracts blessing. The more humble you become, the more magnetic you become . . . When you humble yourself, the Holy Spirit does the heavy lifting. Humility allows God to do what God does. Humility is the key to spiritual authority: more humility [equals] more authority.
>
> If you want to see God move in powerful ways, all you need to do is stay out of God's way. How? Humility! Staying on your knees is the way to stay out of the way! Or to say it another way, humility is the best way to get out of the way of what God wants to do.
>
> God can accomplish more in one day than you can accomplish in a thousand years, but you've got to posture yourself in humility. You've got to stay humble, stay hungry. Getting on your knees is the surest and fastest and truest way to get where God wants you to go. Hit your knees![13]

Let me offer two examples of how humility can change individual hearts and even society at large.

One incredible story is found in the Book of Mormon. The Book of Mormon is a thousand-year history (approximately 600 BCE to 400 CE) of peoples who inhabited the Americas long ago. In this record, there are numerous stories of societies rising and falling—usually coinciding with the Pride Cycle. One subgroup known as the Anti-Nephi-Lehies had separated from the larger group known as the Lamanites, choosing to stop warring and live a more peaceful existence alongside the Nephites. These two groups, the Lamanites and the Nephites, had fought with each other for generations.

At this particular time, the Lamanites were more aggressive, though the two groups alternated in their desires for peace. The Lamanites were angry with their brothers the Anti-Nephi-Lehies, because they had become friendly with the Nephites and had converted to God.

It says in the record that "their hatred became exceedingly sore . . . and they took up arms against [them]." The people of Anti-Nephi-Lehi would not defend themselves or "make preparations for war." They described themselves as having been forgiven by God for their "many sins and murders [committed in the past], and that He had "taken away the guilt from [their] hearts." Rather than fight and "stain [their} swords with the blood of [their] brethren," they did bury their weapons "deep in the earth."

> Now when the people (of Anti-Nephi-Lehi) saw (the Lamanites) coming, they went out to meet them, and prostrated themselves before them . . . and began to call on the name of the Lord; and thus they were in this attitude when the Lamanites began to fall upon them, and . . . slay them with the sword. And thus without [having] any resistance, they [the Lamanites] did slay a thousand and five of them; and we know that they are blessed, [and] have gone to dwell with their God.
>
> When the Lamanites saw that their brethren would not flee from the sword . . . but . . . would lie down and perish, and [praise] God even in the very act of perishing . . . the Lamanites . . . did [cease] from slaying them; and . . . [their hearts did swell for] . . . their brethren who had fallen under the sword. [It was then] that they threw down their weapons of war, and they would not take them again, for they were stung for the murders which they had committed; . . . [then] the people of God were joined that day by more than the number who had been slain.[14]

Imagine that miracle of watching those who had taken innocent lives become humbled by a mighty change in their hearts.

What would happen in our society if we possessed a character as true as the Anti-Nephi-Lehies?

This next story is one we are all familiar with. It's the amazing methods of Martin Luther King Jr. and how he affected change. The process was effective because it was fashioned in the mode of Ghandi. Nonviolent and peaceful protests are a very potent way to bring about change. They capture the minds and sympathies of both the observers, as well as the participants.

Most of us recognize injustice and inequality and King's approach didn't repel; it drew others to the movement. The path can be long and hard, but ultimately "right" does prevail. It's rather interesting that King's marches and protests used many of the virtues we've been alluding to: hope, patience, authenticity, courage, and long-suffering. The sought-for changes, though difficult and time-intensive, eventually brought real, lasting change. Violence and mayhem, the antithesis of humility, only result in more of the same.

It's our own personal decision making that ultimately results in improving or worsening our character. That very process (of pain and suffering), and the tension in our souls, helps us to grow. Humility is indeed a virtue and a key for steady personal development. Humility is accepting the struggle and a willingness to stay the course. When we deny, repress, rationalize, or use other defense mechanisms, we choose an alternate reality, and this stymies the change process.

Rick Warren said it well: "It's not that we [need to] think less of ourselves but rather that we think of ourselves less."[15]

This is humility and the gateway to internal change and the blessings that follow.

The Fruits of Humility

The word *beatus* in Latin means "to be fortunate," or "to be happy or blessed." The Beatitudes contain some rather difficult but amazing laws for living. They offer promised blessings when we show love and humility toward God and treat others similarly.

Several of the Beatitudes *indirectly* make references to humility:

1. *Blessed are they that mourn: for they shall be comforted.* (Someone who believes, and who mourns and is sorrowful, is usually humble).

2. *Blessed are they which do hunger and thirst after righteousness: for they shall be filled.* (One who is teachable and chooses to do good is generally humble).

3. *Blessed are the merciful: for they shall obtain mercy.* (A person who forgives and offers mercy is humble).

4. *Blessed are the pure in heart: for they shall see God.* (A person seeking to be moral and pure is humble).

5. *Blessed are they which are persecuted for righteousness' sake: for theirs is the kingdom of heaven.* (A person with high integrity, who out of principle doesn't fight back (such as the Anti-Nephi-Lehies), is full of humility).

Several have a *direct* relationship to the importance of being humble:

1. *Blessed are the poor in spirit: for theirs is the kingdom of heaven.* (This is someone who realizes their true identity and is not prideful but authentically real and humble).

2. *Blessed are the meek: for they shall inherit the earth.* (In Greek, these are the gentle, forgiving, benevolent; in Hebrew, it suggests these are the humble and those who have suffered).

3. *Blessed are the peacemakers: for they shall be called the children of God.* (What would we do without all those who have sought for peace, who have staved off conflict and war in families, cities, and Nations? The Ghandis, the Martin Luther Kings, the Mother Teresas, the Dalai Lamas, the Desmond Tutus, the known and the unknown peacegivers of the world?[16]

These teachings exhort the follower to seek humility. The virtue of humility seems to be at the center of everything that Christ said and did. He often told those that witnessed miracles (another sign of humility), "see that you tell no man."[17]

He taught those who listened to Our Father, how to live in love and peace, how to refrain from judging others, and how to find their way back home (eternal life). Most importantly, He was sent to sacrifice His life for each of us through the infinite Atonement. His birth was of humble circumstances, born in a stable among the animals, though He stated during His arrest in the Garden of Gethsemane, "Thinkest thou that I cannot now pray to my Father, and he shall presently give me more than twelve legions of angels?"[18]

He showed us that suffering, an important aspect of humility, was necessary and refining to the human soul. He resisted using the power of force, and instead chose the power of the word and the power of love as he "went about doing good."[19]

He taught that persuasion, long-suffering, gentleness, and meekness are the powers that truly change minds and hearts.

Humility, at the end of the day, is about submission—submitting our will (the only thing we really have to give) to Him and the Father, the creator of all things. In doing so, They offer us a peace that "surpasses all understanding!"[20]

Chapter 5

Repentance

"Repentance must dig the foundations, but holiness shall erect the structure, and bring forth the top-stone. Repentance is the clearing away of the rubbish of the past temple of sin; holiness builds the new temple which the Lord our God shall inherit. Repentance and desires after holiness never can be separated." —Charles H. Spurgeon

What Is Repentance?

When we want or need to change, when something inside us doesn't feel right, we can do any number of things. We can deny, suppress, or run from it. We can blame others, get depressed, or self-medicate. We can journal and do our own analysis; this can be helpful. Processing our problems is enhanced with a mentor, a guide, someone to talk to. If we believe we've violated our deepest self, which involves something of the soul, we might consider addressing things more spiritually. Taking this course is called repentance.

"No evil dooms us hopelessly except the evil we love, and desire to continue in, and make no effort to escape from."[1]

We don't talk much about repentance anymore or how the process works. After all, it is a religious practice, and we've become less religious; some say we're more spiritual. Religion involves practices that some believe aren't helpful, since these practices are man-made. Repentance, however, is a process taught by all faiths and traditions. The actions may vary, but the aim is similar.

"Before I can live with other folks, I've got to live with myself. The one thing that doesn't abide by majority rule is a person's conscience."[2]

Repentance is hard stuff. To begin with, it's hard to change, and repentance is all about change. It's been said that people don't like to change or be changed. I know that's true for me.

Working through some issues can take months, and truth be told, even years. Repentance is a change of heart and mind, a "turning away from," if you will.

People repent in their own way and do so because they feel moved upon to change. What they are in, what they are experiencing, is no longer tolerable. Mostly what they're seeking is relief.

If this sounds like you, chances are you've gone through some or maybe all the steps of change. (We'll go through these steps in a moment.) We don't always do them in order, and we'll likely repeat them as we go deeper in the repentance process. It's not easy to address the weightier matters of life.

"It is not the absence of sin but the grieving over it which distinguishes the child of God from empty professors."[3]

Repentance has always been associated with our spiritual selves. God has commanded all humankind to repent, because by our very nature, we all fall short. When we repent, we grow, and that's what any good father wants for his children. When we repent, we are showing our faith in a being who can help us. God is the creator of all things in the universe, including our unique, individual spirits. The spirit is the part of us (the invisible matter) that is housed by our body, like a hand in a glove. Our spirit is intelligence. It senses the world through our thoughts and feelings and can become wounded when we rebel or stray from Him by not living in accordance with universal or natural laws (i.e., the commandments). We regain or receive peace as we turn back and place ourselves in alignment with Him.

The Father has a plan for us, and in that plan He can make more of us than we can by ourselves. When we listen intently, we receive light and truth. Acknowledging Him is recognizing that He will, through divine law (underscored with love), provide direction and a course for our true happiness.

"Wickedness never was happiness."[4]

When we repent or change, we reattach ourselves with His spirit and mentorship.

Repentance has also been explained as feeling a sincere regret or remorse for one's actions. Most of the time, we feel bad because we've violated our own personal ethics or morality. If we fail to act on the impulses to change our ways by rationalizing them, these spiritual inclinations often weaken or dissipate altogether. The suggestion to change or do better comes from our conscience, which guides us toward light and truth.

Think of the things you've really felt bad about. You promised yourself (and maybe God) that you would never do them again. And then you did them, again, and then again. This can leave you feeling less than whole, maybe even lousy.

Sometimes we change and change for good. Clearly, it's due to our motivation, effort, and inspiration, and let's not leave out the part God plays, I can't tell you how many addicts have told me that only by a higher power was their recovery made possible. It's not that they became perfect or never relapsed. They did, and so do we. It's that the time and space of sobriety that was carved out was only possible by His grace. Their stories are usually accompanied with a smile and a deep reflective look, if only for a moment. This kind of change is a wonderful thing and nothing less than a miracle and not fully explained by any real logic.

"The heavens will not be filled with those who never made mistakes but with those who recognized that they were off course and who corrected their ways to get back in the light . . ."[5]

There are certainly degrees of wrongdoing when we betray the tenets of our own morality. Self-compassion is a good thing. We may need to take the long view on some of our misbehavior. We are humans in the process of becoming, and it may take larger or longer portions of our lives in order to overcome some things. Huck Finn said it best: "you can't pray a lie," explaining our hearts need to be in it if we're to realize any real change.

There has been plenty written about what repentance means, most of it sourced from holy scripture, then conveyed to the masses by religious men. A well-known theologian and writer of seventeenth-century

England wrote a book titled *The Doctrine of Repentance*.[6] What he taught follows closely with the steps below. They are what many learned while attending Sunday School classes. The following ideas are widely accepted as the essence of traditional Christian repentance. They are logical, instructive, and somewhat linear. If this is a stretch for you, open your minds to the intent therein. They really do contain the elements of personal, meaningful change, whether of a spiritual or temporal nature.

1. **Recognition.** Simply put, this is an awareness that we are in error. It is here that we become conscious that our life is out of sorts, our inner peace fragmented. It's a type of cognitive dissonance. We find ourselves with conflicting attitudes, beliefs, or behaviors, which results in a feeling of mental discomfort. What we've been doing does not fit with who we are or want to be. A course correction is needed to restore inner balance.

2. **Sorrow.** If recognition is a time of knowing, sorrow is a time of feeling. We feel bad inside for what we've done. The degree of pain may range from minor distress to overwhelming heartache and suffering. We have regret and empathy for the person or thing we've offended. If there is genuine sorrow, it will humble us. It will bring us to a sense of our own imperfections and limitations. We want to help the other who we've wounded, and that includes the self. We seek relief, because we want to do and feel better. Pain is a motivator, an indicator, that something internal needs to change. We can honor the process, by acknowledging our feelings and allowing them to be a catalyst toward the healing that is needed.

3. **Confession.** There is a certain amount of relief that comes by talking to someone about our problems. Some go to a therapist, or a priest or religious leader, whereas others turn to a trusted friend. Confession, however, is more than talking about one's problems. It's an earnest admission and taking responsibility. It's the process of coming fully clean, telling the truth to whomever or wherever it's needed. It's squaring our shoulders and facing things head-on. It's bearing our soul to the One who always knows and is never

deceived. In the AA tradition, step five teaches us that a confession is an admission to God, to ourselves, and to another human of the exact nature of our wrongs. Voluntary confession is best when it comes from the heart. Coerced confession will likely be "put on" as the motives for change are conflicted. A meaningful confession will greatly impact the cleansing effect.

4. **Abandonment.** It's here that we abandon the sin or behavior. Thomas Watson said, "True repentance, like aqua fortis [nitric acid] eats asunder the iron chain of sin."[7] We don't want the pain anymore that comes with the burden of sin. Feeling delivered, we want to honor the one who helped rescue us. The scriptures talk of this person becoming a "new creature"[8] with a changed disposition. He goes on to say, "I will remove their heart of stone and give them a heart of flesh."[9] We've all likely asked, "Is that kind of change really possible? Can we be reborn, in a sense?" This is not about perfection with never a slip or a slide. That is not humanly possible. What it is about, however, is the heart and a diminishing appetite to do harm or be hurtful, both with things that hurt others or ourselves. With faith, effort, and God's grace, the desire to abandon our darker self is possible.

5. **Restitution.** The focus of making things right (better) for the one who was injured. In AA language, steps eight through nine advise us to make a list of the persons we've harmed, and then be willing to make amends, except when doing so would somehow injure that person or others. Sometimes it is better to leave things where they are and not rehash or revisit them. Every person and situation will be different. Restoring what was taken from the other demonstrates that the offender's efforts are authentic. Restitution may not fully fix things, but it can hasten healing and help bring closure. With this, some justice is delivered, with a bonus being the offender's self-image is improved. If there are material things that need restorations, do them. A letter or a face-to-face meeting can be very beneficial too. The best outcomes will use sound judgement with the aim always to heal and not to harm.

6. **Living Anew.** If the process of change is real and meaningful, we will be lifted up. We are different now, changed, better than we were. We are not perfect, still far from it. But perhaps, as like the layers of an onion, we are learning, growing, gaining a little wisdom, and a deeper awareness of ourselves and life. Through the process of seeing and feeling another's pain and choosing to offer love and healing, something new has been created to replace what was previously dark and dying.

What Will Challenge Our Desire to Repent?

We live in a world of sin and decadence. Anything and everything goes, if you want it. I grew up in a pretty sheltered existence. The community was small, rural, agricultural, and Christian. There were bars and immorality lurking, but sin wasn't visually common or blatant. Being human and prone to error, the opportunity is always there. I didn't travel much until I was an adult. I remember the shock of seeing handbills littered on the streets of LA and Las Vegas advertising for any and all kinds of sexual experiences. There are vastly different worlds all within our own country. Now with the internet and information age, that worldliness is more accessible. Sex in all its forms is in demand, anonymous, at anyone's beck and call.

The world would tell you to partake of the smorgasbord before you. Life is to be lived, enjoyed, and indulged in. Don't be uptight, a prude, or follow those rules. Whose rules are they anyway? It's your life and yours to do as you wish.

> And there shall be many which shall say: Eat, drink and be merry, for tomorrow we die; and it shall be well with us . . . nevertheless, fear God—he will justify in committing a little sin . . . [if] we are guilty,[He] will beat us with a few stripes, and at last we shall be saved in the kingdom of God . . . and others will he [Satan] pacify, and lull them away into carnal security, that they will say: All is well in Zion . . . [and] others he flattereth away, and telleth them there is no hell; and he saith unto them: I am no devil."[10]

There is so much in the world that is good and worthy of our time and energy. But we ought to beware of the Sirens of our world that are attractive, intoxicating, and addictive (i.e. sexual impropriety and excess, drug and alcohol escapism, gambling, excesses in sports, or other kinds of entertainment).

In Homer's *The Odyssey,* Ulysses and his men are well aware of the Sirens—dangerous creatures who lure sailors with their enchanting music and singing to shipwreck on the rocky coasts of their islands. To save themselves, Ulysses had the crew tie him up, then orders them to block their ears to prevent them from hearing the Siren's singing.[11]

Like in the world of *The Odyssey,* each of us have our own Sirens. Learning and living by virtuous principles, and then repenting as we need help, will grant us freedom and help us cope with the increasing darkness and challenges of the world.

How to Make Repentance a Useful Principle

We all are fallible and subject to error as human beings, and there are, of course, different kinds of mistakes. Mistakes are those things that we unintentionally do that generally don't have serious consequences and are usually not a moral issue (i.e., speeding ticket, forgetting to pick up your friend from the airport, failure to get a building permit for doing some work in your home, etc.). They may or may not be prohibited or of a legal nature.

Sin means 'to miss the mark.' It can refer to doing something against God or against a person (Exodus 10:16), doing the opposite of what is right (Galatians 5:17), doing something that will have negative results (Proverbs 24:33–34), and failing to do something you know is right (James 4:17)."[12]

Sin is more serious. These indiscretions tend to have greater societal disapproval. They are violations of the deeper natural or spiritual laws that are God-given. It's not that everything can be defined in any precise way.

We know right from wrong; at the end of the day our conscience offers us guidance.

In corporate America, we've become inundated with goals and improvement programs to increase efficiency, engagement, and employee purpose and meaning.

The SMART method is all about personal growth and development, meant to help both the employee and ultimately the corporate bottom line.

In our own lives, we need help to change and find personal reformation from time to time. Maybe we can stop getting so hung up on the word sin, and begin to see it (repentance) as an invitation to do more, to feel more, and to become more of a better person. It's a mental, emotional, and spiritual process that uses reflection, self-honesty, a desire to change by taking steps toward having accountability to yourself and God and another person, which can be helpful.

Seeing a counselor, going to visit a priest or pastor, talking to your spouse or significant other, all these can advance our desire for wellness and a deeper felt change. Ultimately turning to and counseling with God, our higher power, is at the front and center of it all. If you're not sure about God, pull out your journal (or create one) and start the process. Follow the steps above; I think you'll find them helpful.

Changing ourselves is not always about addressing sin. Sometimes there is a fine line between seeking personal growth and moral repair. How do you tease out that which is only mental, emotional, or spiritual?

I have used all the methods above: a therapist, a church leader, a spouse, self, and God. At the end of the day, it is a partnership between the two pf you. I have not literally heard the voice of God, but I have seen the effects from counseling with Him. I truly believe He is there for us.

What Are the Fruits of Repentance?

"There is a higher court than the courts of justice and that is the court of conscience. It supersedes all other courts."[13]

I heard an address some years ago about the difference between peace of mind and peace of conscience. It was rather intriguing and worthy of some discussion as we further consider the subject of repentance. Our conscience is essentially our inner voice. It is "feeling" oriented and functions as a guide to our thoughts and choices based on our value system. We all sense right and wrong through our conscience.

Richard G. Scott taught that peace of conscience is a result of living a righteous or more principled life. When we follow natural laws or God's spiritual laws, we are aligned with Him, and thus have peace. These principles are taught in nearly all religions and traditions.

In contrast, peace of mind is the result of the more temporal issues that we face. When the circumstances of our lives are difficult or distressing, we become weighed down, and this affects our thoughts, actions, and emotions. We may even become anxious or depressed. As we resolve or find ways to cope with these matters, our peace is restored once again.

One can have peace of conscience and not have peace of mind but there is rarely peace of mind without peace of conscience.[14]

There are many in our midst who display a quiet dignity and confidence, likely the result of their personal integrity. They may be suffering hardships of health, finances, "wayward" children, even loneliness, but they will have peace of conscience, as they do their best to live an honest, principled life.

Peace of mind is disrupted because we live in an imperfect world, full of things we cannot control. Life's circumstances more often impact our peace of mind. But our internal world that we carry around in our heads is the result of how well we adhere to our principles and ideals. When we live by them and then repent or reform ourselves when we violate them (as we all will do), we will have peace of conscience.

In this book, which is about the fruits of virtue, let me share a little of what's written about the benefits of repentance from Christian scripture:

"Now no chastening for the present seemeth to be joyous, but grievous: nevertheless afterward it yieldeth the peaceable fruit of righteousness unto them which are exercised thereby."[15]

In other words, we suffer from the effects of sin or error, but as we turn back through our own reformation, we experience the fruit of peace. "And now, my brethren, I would that ye should humble yourselves before God, and bring forth fruit meet for repentance, that ye may also enter into that rest."[16] This has reference to the peace we find as we soften our hearts and live in harmony with true principles. This peace can be gifted to us here as well as in the afterlife where we may enjoy His presence.

Chapter 6

Patience

"Patience is the calm acceptance that things can happen in a different order than the one you have in your mind." —David G. Allen

What Is Patience?

Patience is defined as the ability to carry on in the face of provocation, affliction, or pain, without complaining or the loss of temper. It's a willingness to suppress feelings of restlessness or annoyance when confronted with delay. It's more than just enduring but enduring well life's challenges. It's been said,

"A man who masters patience masters everything else."[1]

Of all the virtues, one of the most common that people fall short of is impatience. In fact, people will often freely admit they are lacking in this trait. I know I have. There have been times in my life where impatience was one of my biggest weaknesses. Maybe it's easy to spot in others when it's one of our own. This is one of those qualities you hear others being openly scolded for.

- "You're so impatient."
- "Oh, just calm down, it's not going to take that long!"
- "Why don't you find something else to do for a little while."
- "Don't blame them; can't you see they're doing the best that they can?"

You get the point. We want what we want when we want it!

My mother used to tell my dad how impatient he was when she asked him to watch the grandchildren for a while. Maybe you can recall the impatience expressed by disgruntled family members waiting for their order at the restaurant, or remember "punching it" through a red light, because you didn't want to wait.

My brother's license plate reads I-8-2-W-8 (I hate to wait).

We've become accustomed to the immediate gratification of our needs; where we can quickly pull up the movie of our choice and have our favorite sandwich delivered in only five minutes. We feel we're entitled.

It's harder now to plant and nurture a garden; to hang around a job long enough to see a promotion or raise; to save up for that newer car or bigger house, because we want to have it now. The news cycle moves so fast; everything is at warp speed. It's hard to find patience with everything moving so fast.

I can recall times of showing patience and the times I was lacking in patience.

Perhaps you can recall a memory or two where a lack of patience got you in trouble. I have a long list of being shortsighted and of making impulsive decisions, because I wanted it right then. The experiences of our errors help us develop more patience.

All that glitters is not gold. I have indulged in a few investments (you probably have too) where the salesman promised great returns, but it was imperative you invest now and get in on the ground floor. Remember the IPOs and dot-com businesses of the early 2000s? Most of them fizzled, but you jumped in because that big payoff was coming. Some risk isn't bad, but remembering the growth of most investments will be measured and steady.

I returned as soon as possible to my home after completing a PhD in Psychology, so I could practice with my family who had just built a clinic. By doing so, I missed out on the opportunity for some additional training. Why? Because I was in a hurry to go to work, make some money, build a home, etc. In retrospect, it would have been better to have been less impulsive and more judicious.

I, of course, have many other personal examples, but I won't bore you or embarrass myself!

Don't beat yourself up for being impulsive or for your own miscalculations. It's how we ultimately learn and better decipher future events; thus, we learn what it means to be patient.

The following poem explains how patience teaches us through the pattern of cycles. There's a time for holding back, waiting, and watching. Doing so brings us to the people and the places where we need to be. I think the adage "be still" and listening within is very pertinent:

> The world of nature exists
> within a larger pattern of cycles,
> such as day and night
> and the passing of the seasons.
>
> The seasons do not push one another;
> neither do clouds race the wind across the sky;
> all things happen in good time;
> Everything has a time to rise, and a time to fall.
>
> Whatever rises, falls,
> and whatever falls shall rise again;
> that is the principle of cycles.
>
> Patience is power;
> with time and patience,
> the mulberry leaf becomes silk.[2]

I served a voluntary two-year mission here in the United States for my church. The rules and regulations were somewhat rigorous: no newspaper or radio or TV, no dating, up at six and in bed by ten, no hanging out in the apartment to just pass time. We were out teaching and trying to help people, twelve-hour days, six-and-a-half days of the week. The experience was exhausting and fulfilling all at the same time. This was my third attempt to serve, and because of some patience I finally had a successful outcome.

I went to school for a long, long time—nearly ten years beyond high school. This required some patience.

What Will Challenge Our Patience?

There are those things in our lives that are really big and life-changing. These are what some might call watershed experiences. The other smaller things can test our patience, but they're just small potatoes (i.e., babysitting, waiting in a restaurant, investments maturing, and red lights). These things just pale in comparison to the things we refer to as matters of the heart, the ones that are grueling, gut-wrenching, and sometimes filled with moments of fear.

They seem to pass slowly, and we might even feel that patience is being forced upon us, because we want to solve them now. We learn haltingly there are no quick, easy, solutions. We find that patience and our faith is all we have in these moments, which can last for months or even years. During those difficult times, it feels as if they'll never end.

I know you've had them. If not, they are coming. It's those things that test our mettle, and it seems at times our mettle isn't very strong. But somehow, we do survive. We get through them, and perhaps learn powerful lessons of patience. It's been said that "we survive every moment but the last one."[3] Some consolation that is!

I remember my wife and I were married about a year and decided it was time to start a family. We were in our mid-twenties, so we thought we were mature enough. My wife became pregnant and we were really excited. About nine weeks later, she miscarried. It was more than eleven years later that we finally received a child—through adoption. Though there were painful times, such as Mother's Day celebrations with family, we just soldiered on. Patience is a maturing, sobering, "face the reality of life" kind of thing. When our children eventually came to us, there was a special kind of excitement and process to go through. If you think nine months is long, we waited about three years (after filing papers) to receive each of our children.

When is patience and fortitude not needed? Think of your children, your marriage, or any significant relationship you're invested in. How about your health or your occupation, searching for purpose and meaning, addictions or dependencies, or financial struggles? Maybe you've had a combination of these issues and many others.

Are you learning patience?

Life is not always what we want it to be, it just is!

Patience is to stay with things when the course is unclear and the outcome unsure. Usually the most difficult times are the ones that involve the lessons of relationships, especially the ones we have with ourselves.

When the going gets tough, where are we to be found? Are we "emotionally present" and available to those who need us?

The following is a poignant account of a friend from the larger neighborhood where I live. She expresses, how in difficult times, and in sometimes short supply, how important patience is.

At fifty-five, I believe I have been through many crises. I had a father who suffered a brain tumor during my childhood years (I am his legal guardian now). Closer family members that I love have experienced childhood sexual abuse and alcoholism. I personally experienced a miscarriage, organ failure, a premature birth, I died and came back. I had cancer twice and a bone marrow transplant. I know many people have experienced these things and worse. We've all had things we experienced together as a people. 9/11 was hard. War is hard. Financial or reputation ruin is hard. Death of a loved one is hard.

I have learned that during these times, our strengths or weaknesses can be amplified. It has helped me in muddling through these times with others, if I can identify strengths in others and become vocal about them.

I've learned that at times, myself and others can become hypercritical and controlling when we are scared. When others have been this way with me, I just want to be far away from them. But I've learned to try to do the opposite. To instead, STAY with them, allow them control as long as it doesn't escalate into the abuse of anyone. Be the voice of calm, and assurance, and especially validate them.

So, my advice now—with the crisis, where our homes may be a hot mess of emotion, STAY. Give yourself (and others in your care) timeouts but STAY. Especially don't turn your back on the children that you are responsible for. STAY with them. Give it all you've got to have faith and endure. Better days are coming, and you will be glad you did."[4]

My wife and I had a wearying experience with our children a few years back, particularly in their dangerous use of drugs and alcohol. Sometimes we enabled them and responded in the same ineffective ways over and over again. Sometimes, we didn't have our own act together so that our children could receive a consistent message. Sometimes, the systems we reached out to just weren't helpful. Systems after all, are made up of people who are fallible and imperfect themselves. Each of us are ultimately responsible and an agent to ourselves. In many instances we cause our own pain and grief, while at the same time being the only ones that can fix it.

Whatever the problem we face, they all take energy, time, and usually lots of patience.

How to Make Patience Your Own

I believe we were meant to struggle and fail, so when we finally get it—and we will—those lessons and their meanings will run deep within us.

The point to be made is that there are painful things in life, and they take time to work themselves out. We will not, nor should we, take our hands off the wheel, for easy solutions to problems rarely exist. We must grapple in finding what works, and that's often through the methods of trial and error. A problem that may be harder for one may be easier for another and vice versa. It's interesting how often others believe they have cookie-cutter solutions for our problems. They likely mean well, but these are things only we can fix. Patience!

Thankfully, the law of consequences is ever present and helps us out, if we let it. Consequences are a friend to patience. They keep things real and moving forward, if only slowly. Sometimes we just need to get out of our own way. More often than not we aggravate the problem by "rolling in the cactus." This is when we focus on our suffering, rather than continue to search for solutions.

When we begin to follow through within the limits and parameters that are set, amazing things will happen. During the riots of May 2020, it was interesting to see mayors in large US cities set curfew times for those protesting. But when the time came, there was no enforcement. When curfews were finally enforced, there was vast improvement on the streets.

"Be patient. Everything will come together. Whatever you are waiting for is on its way" (Ralph Smart).

Almost always there are lessons to be learned, regardless of the role you're in, such as occur between parents and children. The consequences from actions taken, becomes a type of dance with lessons to be learned by all. It takes time, patience and ideally a deep involvement called love. This was certainly true regarding the experiences with our son.

Our son was wrecking his life, I will spare you most of the details. "Wrecking" is an appropriate metaphor for describing his last few years, before he left home. You see, he wrecked the car several cars. He turned the car on its side when he hit a snow embankment; he then drove the same car down into a canal from a road that was poorly lit; it all climaxed when he finally hit a deer at a high rate of speed which resulted in the car being totaled. He was "using" and had impaired judgment. We wondered when we would get that call in the middle of the night that he hadn't made it. He moved out for a time when we asked him to. He returned— with certain stipulations. Things regressed like before. When police came to our home with a search warrant, that was "game over!" We had survived; though our patience was worn thin, it had brought us through. We had stayed the course, offering all the options possible. Now, the ball was in his court. He is now living out of state, growing up some, seeing things more clearly. He has a reasonable chance of making it. We love him.

One morning, I was up on the floor of the hospital visiting patients. Sometimes you feel almost drawn to a room. This seemed to be the case for me, and after entering one particular room, I found an older female who had been admitted over the weekend. She had not felt well-cared for up to this point and was anxiously waiting to see her doctors and get their recommendations. She seemed lonely, yet she was receptive to someone taking a genuine interest in her. She quickly opened up without much prompting. I learned she had survived ovarian cancer some years earlier. She had all of her female organs removed and was told she had a good chance of recovery, which she achieved. She came to the hospital at this time due to some symptoms that concerned her. When the hospitalist received the scans, he was candid with her. Her tumor had returned, and she didn't have long to live.

She desperately needed to talk and to open up about her feelings.

She had spent all her adult life in the insurance industry in a large Midwestern city. She'd enjoyed her life and the privilege of traveling a great deal. She was religious and said she had tried to live a good life. She had dated but never found anyone she truly loved. Never marrying or having children was a great disappointment. She had moments of despair, crying out to God many times, "Why have I never found anyone to marry? Is there something wrong with me?" She explained, "I just never met the right one or really fell in love." One night after an evening out, she returned to her apartment alone and found herself crying once again. She recalled, "I remember my little dog was licking my face as I cried once again, 'Why have you never brought anyone into my life?' She heard a voice briefly but distinctly, "Because he's here waiting for you!" She reiterated, "This part of life has never been easy, but since this experience, I've never felt as lonely or forsaken. I have something to look forward to."

Sometimes, we may need to wait with patience, if even for a lifetime.

I've experienced several life-threatening illnesses during my own life. One came as a junior in high school, when I was diagnosed with osteo-myelitis, a bone infection that required being hospitalized for nearly eight weeks. I missed much of my senior year, including participating in sports. I was an impatient inpatient, but I learned to endure.

At age fifty, I was doing push-ups and experienced what are called par-oxysmal symptoms. I would describe the symptoms as sensations similar to what an electric shock might feel like as it pulses through your body. A week later, I was diagnosed with MS from an MRI and spinal tap used to confirm suspicions. This was indeed a jolt to my psyche in all ways. I could hardly move without triggering pseudo-seizures. I prayed and sought blessings and exercised all the faith I had—that I might be spared from such a debilitating disease. I changed my diet, meditated, and used visualization, among other things. And I kept praying, as did others in my behalf. Slowly over a period of months, I saw improvement. As the years passed I felt better and better.

What Are the Fruits of Patience?

Patience will bring good things into our life if we'll pause, wait, and listen. The following poem illustrates the struggle of life as we grow and learn, hopefully with patience.

Stumbling...   ...Healing
Falling...   Standing...
Bleeding...   Kneeling...
This is how we grow![5]

"He that can have patience can have what he will."[6]

"Trust the process. Your time is coming. Just do the work and the results will handle themselves."[7]

The Virtues of Character

Morality, Self-Mastery, Courage

The virtues of character are about developing and following the inner compass. This compass provides direction for the moral and sometimes difficult decisions we all will encounter. As we make choices consistent with our conscience, we experience joy and peace. When these values are internalized, we're able to advocate for our principles, for others, and honorable causes in the community.

Chapter 7

Morality

"Freedom exercised without the tempering of wisdom and the guidance of ethics is freedom gone rogue. And freedom gone rogue is no longer freedom. Rather, it is the rather effective method by which we've now chosen to destroy ourselves." —Craig D. Lounsbrough

What Is Morality?

Alexis de Tocqueville was a French aristocrat, diplomat, political scientist, and historian. He was interested in the factors that led to improved living standards and social conditions of those in Western societies. He was a passionate lover of liberty, the law, and the respect for human rights. He traveled America for the intent to discover its success:

> I sought for the greatness and genius of America in her commodious harbors and her ample rivers—and it was not there . . . in her fertile fields and boundless forests and it was not there . . . in her rich mines and her vast world commerce—and it was not there . . . in her democratic Congress and her matchless Constitution—and it was not there. Not until I went into the churches of America and heard her pulpits aflame with righteousness did I understand the secret of her genius and power. America is great because she is good, and if America ever ceases to be good, she will cease to be great.[1]

After much observation and analysis, one conclusion he reached was: "Liberty cannot be established without morality, nor morality without faith."[2]

What does it mean to be a moral person? And whose morality are we talking about?

Does being moral actually make a difference in one's own life and in the larger community? If so, what exactly are the benefits, and how are they manifest?

Are moral principles broad and encompassing enough that most people would recognize them as principles of truth; principles that work for the welfare of all people?

Are moral principles intuitive, placed inside us by the Creator? If so, does that make it easier to be moral?

Is morality a manifestation of natural law that was discussed in this book's introduction?

Are all of these things part of God's manual—the principles for living a happy and prosperous life?

How does morality correspond with our thoughts, our conscience, and actions?

In recent years, a newer model to explain moral development has emerged. It is called Moral Foundations Theory, and it is based on the work of Jonathon Haidt and his colleagues. Anyone in psychology or education will remember learning about the theories of cognitive and moral development as espoused by Jean Piaget (1930s) and later Lawrence Kohlberg (1950s). For me, these theories didn't explain things fully. They were theoretical, and something seemed to be missing.

In Haidt's model of moral development, it is both logical and seems intuitively better at explaining things. Of course, science is always evolving to find the truth that exists in our world. Haidt's system involves six innate moral foundations that exist on a continuum. They are:

- **Care/Harm:** this component may be the most foundational. As human beings or mammals, we have attachment systems. We feel for our offspring and others and naturally dislike seeing others hurting or in pain. Thus, we tend toward exhibiting the virtues of kindness, gentleness, and nurturance.

- **Fairness/Cheating:** this element relates to the process of seeking to be part of a fair world. It creates a natural desire for justice, rights, and autonomy.

- **Loyalty/Betrayal:** this component is related to our history of affiliating in groups that have a common cause or purpose, including that of survival. It naturally connects to virtues of patriotism and sacrificing for the group that one is a part of.

- **Authority/Subversion:** this element has been shaped by a history of ranked social interactions. It's concerned with who the leaders and followers are, and includes how or why we yield to recognized authority and show respect for tradition.

- **Sanctity/Degradation:** this component was shaped by the psychology of disgust and contamination. It includes the religious notions of striving to live in an elevated, less carnal, more noble way. It underlies the widespread idea that the body is a temple that can be desecrated by immoral activities and contaminants (an idea not unique to religious traditions).

- **Liberty/Oppression:** this element is about why people react to and resent others who try to dominate them and restrict their liberty. Its intuitions are often in tension with those of the authority foundation. The hatred of bullies and dominators motivates people to come together in solidarity to oppose or take down the oppressor.[3]

The model that undergirds our American society is commonly known as the Judeo-Christian ethic and uses the Ten Commandments as its foundation. It's less of a theoretical model and more about what many have been taught as the basis for morality. It is referred to more in the church now and less in the public square (as it once was). It is the basis for much of our legal system.

A third strong influence shared by all faith traditions is what is essentially described as the Golden Rule: "Do unto others as you would want them to do unto you." I remember this being taught and referenced much by my schoolteachers through the 1960s when I was in the elementary grades.

These were strong influences for many, as we were taught and formulated our own moral framework for living life. Are our children being taught these and other similar principles as important contributions for moral guidance and direction?

The base word for morality is moral. Morals have been defined as the prevailing standards of behavior that enable people to live cooperatively in groups. It is what societies approve of—of what is right and acceptable. Morals are often taught and passed from one generation to the next. They are God-given, compatible with natural law, and often transcend time and culture.

Think of your conscience—the inner voice that whispers to you when you're facing challenging decisions or choices. It helps you determine what is right and wrong particularly in a so-called progressive world where everything seems turned upside down.

What happened to objective truth versus the current rationalizations of situation ethics?

Today, the "hot button" moral issues are ones of racism and social justice, sexual orientation, and political correctness. They've been in play for several generations, with their origins found in the issues of racism and segregation, the sexual revolution, feminism, equal rights, etc. When I was very young, the traditional moral teachings were based on conventionality, hard work, honesty, patriotism, and respecting authority. By the late 60s, everything was in question. Some of these things needed to be challenged and changed.

Slavery, not immoral to those who practiced it at the time, was eventually seen by the masses as a wicked and abominable practice.

Now there is an attack on old men, particularly old white men. Patriarchy, seen in the past as a cultural norm, became viewed as oppressive and antiquated. I remember as a child that the vast majority of women stayed home rather than enter the work force. Most didn't feel deprived, abused, or thwarted. It was how the system and economy worked; perhaps the downside was its inflexibility. With the family structure changing (more single-parent homes) and an emphasis on equality, and the increasing difficulty in making ends meet, women went to work. They needed to.

Today, there is far more equality. Not surprisingly, women are found in slightly higher numbers than men in both law and medical schools and make up nearly half of all graduating with MBA's.

As improvements were identified and changed in the area of human relations, in many ways, the American experiment rendered more good for more people than any other system in the world. That's why people so fervently try to get in. Our way of life is built on opportunity, hard work, natural law, and traditional morality . Our founders believed the system was built for a moral people, the only basis on which it could thrive.

The Founders stated in the Declaration of Independence that we "are endowed by [our] Creator with certain unalienable rights, that among these are life, liberty, and the pursuit of happiness." The Founders further stated they were qualified to declare this based on "the laws of nature and . . . [that] nature's God entitle[d] them." Think about that for a moment and try to gather the deeper meaning. Suffice it to say, there are principles and order in the universe, and we are a fundamental part of that design. It's how things were created, it's how they work.

The Constitution or system was set up so we'd continually seek for "a more perfect union, establish justice, insure domestic tranquility . . . promote the general welfare and secure the blessings of liberty for ourselves and our posterity." All of this has been a process pursued over time. It's been a collective effort, achieved through a representative form of government, not by mob rule or would-be kings or bureaucrats.

Our Bill of Rights enumerates some of those privileges and helps us to stay free. Those inalienable rights contribute to morality in a big way. It assures we can worship, speak, write, assemble, and defend ourselves; to live our lives in the way we choose—so long as we refrain from harming others and/or infringing on their liberties.

What Are the Challenges in Being Moral?

When I grew up, nearly all young males were in, or had an exposure to, the Boy Scouts of America. It was as American as mom and apple pie. There was the Girl Scout organization for girls; that seemed fair. Boy Scouts was a source for teaching moral principles to young males. Moral principles, ideally, would come first from the home and from the example of parents. Scouting was an adjunct and did a lot of good.

The Scout Law taught us to be "Trustworthy, loyal, helpful, friendly, courteous, kind, obedient, cheerful, thrifty, brave, clean and reverent." These were seemingly universal. I thought they were all good things, so how did the world turn upside down?

The Scout Oath said: "On my honor I will do my best to do my duty to God and my country and to obey the Scout Law; to help other people at all times; to keep myself physically strong, mentally awake, and *morally straight.*"

- In 2013, the 1,400 members of the National Council of the Boy Scouts of America voted to lift the ban of letting openly gay individuals into the Scouts. Openly gay adults were still forbidden to be leaders.

- In 2014, Pascal Tessier became the first known openly gay Boy Scout to become an Eagle Scout.

- In 2015, Tessier became the first openly gay adult Boy Scout to be hired as a summer camp leader.

- Later in 2015, the BSA National Executive Board ratified a resolution that removed the national restriction on openly gay adult leaders and employees.

- In 2017, the BSA Board of Directors unanimously voted on inviting girls into all the Scouting programs.

- On February 18, 2020, the National Boy Scouts of America organization filed for Chapter 11 bankruptcy.[4]

I guess the definition of *morally straight* has changed!

What happened to the observance of natural law or universal morals; ones that previously had broad acceptance across the board? There was a time we didn't question these morals, such as the taking of a life, out-and-out violence, stealing, or adultery. Here are a few examples:

Regarding the *sanctity of life,* it's against the law to take your own life or that of another. But you can abort your own baby during the third trimester in some states. Does a life not matter when it's still in the womb? Are these man-made policies the actions of an increasing moral and just society, or one that focuses more on rights than responsibilities? Should a society legislate or vote to determine when a human life is human? Should this type of morality be up to debate or determined by a judge? I think not!

Some say the unborn child (he or she) is human at conception; others at three, six, or nine months. Should a parent, physician, or anyone have the right to terminate human life? When and for what reasons? What is the value of life, a human life?

Contrast this value of human life with the preservation of a tree, the spotted owl, or some rare marine organism. Areas of the country have ceased being developed, mined, or farmed because of concerns of the impact on native flora, animals, or even microorganisms. All living things contribute to the homeostasis of the environment; we know that's important. But can you really make the case that human life (each and every one of them) is any less sacred? We are stewards of the earth and are tasked to take care of everything, particularly human life. That means one another.

There once was a pervasive belief that *adultery* was wrong. Humans, of course, are imperfect, so they will mess up, but the societal message was that extramarital behavior was wrong. The permissiveness of our day has made it more than tolerated. It's not unusual to find an article in some of the leading magazines lauding the joys of an affair, or how an affair can be psychologically freeing.

The laws in all communities have been clear on *violence* until recently. Assault, battery, and the willful destruction of property has been prohibited and deemed criminal. Those acts usually resulted in charges or an arrest. What was shocking to many Americans was the impotent, and in some cases near silent, response to violence in many US cities during the riots of 2020. Looting, fires, wanton destruction, and attacks on police was rampant and even sanctioned by some community and national leaders.

Is looting and stealing acceptable when done by the poor and marginalized of society? Is violence acceptable when the cause is just? Who will decide that? Who decides that the rights of the victims will be suspended? What made it right to pull down and destroy the property of others simply to make a statement?

Police were hindered from keeping the peace when they were told to "stand down." Law and order didn't coincide with the politics of some governors and mayors. Their actions spoke volumes. It's as if they said, "To hell with the law; we'll let those hellions make their statement."

More and more, the goalposts of right and wrong have shifted. Today, many truths have been replaced by values (or rather preferences) that are subject to what some members of society say is acceptable. Most Americans are put off by the excessiveness of political correctness.[5]

For some, the truths and standards that have served us well and promoted the dignity and respect of all have given way to "this is my truth," which are the values and opinions of the groupthink culture.

Time-tested principles are deeper and eternal. Thomas Paine eloquently wrote: "An army of principles will penetrate where an army of soldiers cannot; it will succeed where diplomatic management would fall: it is neither the Rhine, the Channel, nor the ocean, that can arrest its progress: it will march on the horizon of the world, and it will conquer."[6]

When our personal morality aligns with true moral principles, then we'll be a happier and more just and civil society.

Rishabh R. Dassani describes clearly what happens in society as values no longer reflect the deeper principles: "Values are part of our internal system that guides our behavior, whereas principles are external. Values are subjective, personal, emotional, and arguable, while principles are objective, factual, impersonal, and self-evident because they are indisputable."[7]

How Can You Embrace a Moral Life?

Morality that has origins in God's law and natural law will sustain us in both personal and communal ways.

We have a system of law and order. Without it, there is little safety or security. Safety and security are necessary to transact life with any predictability. Without it, we have anarchy and chaos—not the ingredients for a truly progressing society. Electing people who will focus on relevant and meaningful change when necessary, or using the means of petitioning and referendums; these are the ways to change the system lawfully. Making change in this way is moral and contributes to a moral world.

A conscience comes in many degrees. If our conscience is alive and not seared by neglect, it will guide us in our moral choices. A flickering conscience like a struggling flame can be fashioned into a blaze. Hemingway said,

"So far, about morals, I know only that what is moral is what you feel good after and what is immoral is what you feel bad after."[8]

In the Disney movie *Pinocchio*, Jiminy Cricket acts as a conscience to a wooden puppet named Pinocchio that has been brought to life by the wishes of his carpenter creator Geppetto. Recruited to help Pinocchio, Jiminy Cricket is bestowed the title of "Lord High Keeper of the Knowledge of Right and Wrong." To become real, Pinocchio must prove himself brave, truthful, and unselfish, and be able to tell right from wrong; in other words, he must obtain certain knowledge for his salvation.[9]

We too have a guide that will help us with the small and larger issues we face in life. There is a power that is found within us, placed by the Creator to guide us, His children here on earth.

Like an old-fashioned radio we must turn to the right frequency in order to hear the music. When we follow and honor the still small voice, we will be in tune with our Maker and do what is ultimately the best thing for us, though it may not make sense at the time. That still small voice is a frequency, an energy, and it resonates in us best when we follow God's laws.

Montaigne, one of the most significant philosophers of the French Renaissance and a major influence on scores of great thinkers said, "Were I not to follow the straight road for its straightness, I should follow it for having found by experience that in the end it is commonly the happiest and most useful track."[10]

Should we think we are unique and have an exception—to moral principles? Consider the various reviews of how and why civilizations fail. As they decline, they share some common traits.

After ten years of a relentless research of more than eighty civilizations, J. D. Unwin concluded that "Any human society is free to choose either to display great energy or to enjoy sexual freedom: the evidence is that it cannot do both for . . . (long)."[11]

Historian Arnold Toynbee examined the greatest civilizations of all time, resulting in an exhaustive work published in twelve volumes

(7000 pages), and over a twenty-seven-year period. How long would it take you to read that? I will save you some time and summarize his findings. He found that of twenty-one key nations or societies, nineteen perished not from enemies without but from moral decay within. He discovered that when those societies were most creative and successful, immorality was curbed. They did this by channeling their time and energy into commerce, innovation, and other productive ventures. He concluded that sexual self-constraint was directly related to that nation's strength and accomplishment; a lack of restraint resulted in societal weakness and deterioration.[12]

In the research and writing of *The History of the Decline and Fall of the Roman Empire,* Edward Gibbon found that as Rome declined, sexual immorality became so widespread that it threatened the institution of marriage. There was nothing they did not indulge in or think was a disgrace. The effect on marriage and society was so severe and extensive that Caesar Augustus enacted laws aimed to curb the people's licentiousness. Unfortunately, they didn't work.[13]

According to Gibbon, the Roman Empire succumbed to *barbarian* invasions largely due to the gradual loss of *civic virtue* among its citizens.[14]

You've heard it many times, and it's true, you can't legislate morality. Morality comes from within; from following correct principles (morals) that take hold in the minds and hearts of the people. It helps tremendously when the nation's leaders emphasize morality and are examples themselves.

Randy Alcorn observed after looking at a number of civilizations, that when the ruling group and society as a whole relaxed their code of sexual morality, there was a cultural decline within three generations.[15]

If you look at the decline that transpired in the '60s, '70s, and '80s, you'll realize we are now in the third generation.

The following poem describes the confidence societies often feel about their greatness, especially while they're thriving and well. Yes, societies are living, breathing things, and like humans, think they are invincible. They are, however, destined to crumble and die and end up on the scrap heap of history; particularly when they cause their own implosion through immorality.

> I met a traveller from an *antique* land,
> Who said: Two vast and *trunkless* legs of stone
> Stand in the desert. Near them, on the sand,
> Half sunk, a shattered *visage* lies, whose frown,
> And wrinkled lip, and sneer of cold command,
> Tell that its sculptor well those passions read
> Which yet survive, stamped on these lifeless things,
> The hand that mocked them and the heart that fed;
> And on the pedestal these words appear:
> "My name is *Ozymandias,* king of kings:
> Look on my works, ye Mighty, and despair!"
> Nothing beside remains. Round the decay
> Of that colossal wreck, boundless and bare,
> The lone and level sands stretch far away.[14]

What Are the Fruits of Being Moral?

Jesus told His disciples that if they followed His teachings, they would be made free. They responded," We are Abraham's seed and have never been in bondage to anyone!" A denial or misunderstanding? Jesus replied, "Whoever commits sin is a slave of sin" (John 8:33–34). When we choose to live a moral life, we will find a peace within, the kind only God can give. This is the peace of conscience we discussed earlier.

The conventional wisdom of the ages seems pretty consistent. A moral life may not bring wealth or health, but it will bring about a happiness within.

When we have peace of mind and conscience, we also find goodwill toward others.

We all know the feeling of being "weighed down" from guilt, uncertainty, or despair. By repenting or changing, we are mentally and emotionally lifted up, which creates and restores a sense of freedom. When

Ebenezer Scrooge is redeemed at the end of the story, Charles Dicken's *A Christmas Carol,* his chains are lifted, and he shouts that he feels "light as a feather."

What has happened to right and wrong, today?

Who will stand up and speak with moral authority? Desperate times call for a spiritual leader.

Who is trusted and respected in a way that others may listen? We have the Dalai Lama, the Pope, Christian televangelists, and others. Anciently there were philosophers, sages, even prophets, especially when truth and clarity were needed!

We've been given scripture (believed to be revelation), the inspired words of God delivered to us through chosen ones to speak for Him on earth. These are they who are here today, with both a voice of love and warning: prophets, seers and revelators!

Chapter 8

Self-mastery

"A pivotal spiritual attribute is that of self-mastery—the strength to place reason over appetite. Self-mastery builds a strong conscience. And your conscience determines your moral responses in difficult, tempting, and trying situations." —Elder Russell M. Nelson

What Is Self-mastery?

Morals are the truths that we learn. These are the virtues, natural law, and the commandments. Self-mastery is the practice of the morals and virtues that you've chosen. These are the ones you believe in, the ones you try to live by. It's where the rubber meets the road. If there are morals you've discarded, have you replaced them with something new? With so much truth in the universe, you don't have to live in a vacuum. Life is all about living with our choices and learning from them. It is realizing what is real, finding the courage to live by those principles, then enjoying the attendant blessings of peace and joy.

Developing virtue, a form of self-mastery, comes from the Latin *virtus* meaning manliness. Cicero, a famous Roman statesman and writer, enumerated the cardinal virtues that every man should try to live up to. They included justice, prudence, courage, and temperance. In order to have honor, a Roman man had to live each of these virtues. When Aristotle encouraged men in the ancient world to live "the virtuous life," it was really a call to man up.[1]

"All know the way, but few actually walk it."[2]

I remember being newly married and having a conversation with my father-in-law. We must have been in some deep discussion about life and its meaning. He said, "We are here to learn to control our appetites, passions and desires." At the time—for me, that thought was provocative. The idea wasn't completely new, but I hadn't heard it put quite that way.

What did he actually mean? Why should I even consider these ideas? Is it really our purpose to resist and manage certain impulses; to intentionally pursue a certain way of living? His words took on greater meaning as I encountered different challenges throughout my life.

His words and their meaning are all part of a deeper spiritual pursuit. Are we not souls on a journey for truth, enlightenment, and personal development? Through my own experiences, I've come to believe those notions are true. Perhaps you do as well. Through the teachings of Jesus Christ, we learn that life would be difficult and filled with many challenges. The truths He taught and the choice to follow Him will bring peace of conscience. Any teacher of truth, for that matter, will help its adherents find the benefits that its practice brings.

"The happiness of a man in this life does not consist in the absence but in the mastery of his passions."[3]

What Will Challenge You in Achieving Self-mastery?

Being human, it's natural to seek pleasure. We live in a self-indulgent world. There are infinite choices on what we can do and how to spend our time. Beyond work and sleep, the domain of entertainment is where many go for relief. It's mind-boggling to see the number of movie apps and the variety of sports programming on TV. There is the world of gambling and a smorgasbord of alcohol and drugs (legal and illegal) from which to get high. One can choose their our own way to escape the ever-increasing stresses of the world. Clearly, some choices are better than others.

Some pleasures, however, will become addictive and destructive to our mind, body, and spirit. In choosing the path of self-mastery, we preserve agency and the power to keep our options open. With addiction, we lose the power to choose. Everyone has an Achilles' heel. Be mindful of those tendencies that run in your family (i.e., substance abuse, sexual dependencies, overeating, anger or rage, infidelity, all forms of abuse, etc.). We are ultimately responsible for our actions and the behaviors we choose, but we also carry around the influences from our home, and of course, genetic predispositions. We're going to stumble and fall. Self-mastery is a process (like nearly all of life's processes) of learning and improving as we go. It requires vigilance, effort, honesty, and patience.

"God has entrusted me with myself. No man is free who is not master of himself."[4]

How to Develop Self-mastery in Your Life

Most of us were taught the difference between right and wrong, and hopefully those teachings were modeled for us. We learn by the power of example. When we adopt and live by true principles, such as natural law or following our conscience, our character grows, and we achieve a level of integrity. As we become more disciplined and have someone to account to for our actions, we'll achieve an inner strength. This occurs as we practice personal boundaries resulting in a stronger sense of self.

Self-mastery is the choice to change ourselves for the better. It's deciding to resist those things that stimulate us temporarily but afterward leave us feeling empty. Because the "spirit is willing, but the flesh is weak," it takes time to overcome practices that are harmful. Reading and studying from inspiring words (from any source of authentic truth) will fill your mind with inspiration. It will help lift you up. Having a way to process issues (through a mentor or support group) will help you find strength as well as options for dealing with temptation or weakness.

Meditation and prayer toward a higher power bring results. Their results are rarely immediate, but they will occur!

Think of self-mastery as being like self-discipline. Self-discipline is about controlling or managing ourselves. The root word of discipline is disciple, which means to be a follower or student of a teacher. The best teachers expound truth and light. Once we are taught these principles, it becomes our responsibility to follow them. With natural law as the standard, we become a disciple who lives and follows them, thereby receiving the fruits they produce.

This is not about a total denial of ourselves and our senses. There is much about the world to be enjoyed; like learning, and our choosing things that preserve our agency and peace of mind. Anything that causes conflict, tension, or a weakening of the truths or principles we espouse, become anti-life practices and will rob us of peace and joy.

> Watch your thoughts, they become words;
> watch your words, they become actions;
> watch your actions, they become habits;
> watch your habits, they become character;
> watch your character, for it becomes your destiny.[5]

There are many stories of self-made people. To rise up from having little to achieving great success, takes hard work and discipline— important elements of self-mastery. My neighbor's father came from Holland after the Second World War. He experienced the hardships of the Nazi occupation. He arrived in the US with little money. He settled in California because there was a contingent of Dutch people living in the area. He went to work in a bakery, then after saving a little money, opened his own. He saw that a large bakery in the area was going under and decided to take it over. He worked harder than anyone else and added more space, so he could increase production. When the business climate was no longer favorable, he moved most of the production to Utah. He exercised great discipline in his work and business practices and produced a company that now sells goods nationwide. The company's success was achieved with efficiencies of time, energy, exceptional mental focus, and good decision making, all elements of self-mastery.

One of the great influencers of my life was Jack Wheatley. He was my mission president when I served as a missionary (in my early twenties) for The Church of Jesus Christ of Latter-day Saints. A mission president is chosen to direct missionary work in a specific geographical area, leading and guiding about two hundred (mostly young), missionaries in their proselyting activities.

In writing about Jack, I could have used him as an example in describing nearly all the virtues in this book. I have that much respect for the man. Though he never reached perfection, "he did become a smooth and polished shaft in the quiver of the Almighty."[6]

This can happen for any of us, if we allow Him to fashion us, our wants, and desires.

If any person lived a full and impactful life, it was Jack Wheatley. There are, of course, a number of these incredible human beings. I was fortunate to rub shoulders with this man as a missionary while as a member of his office staff. He had a large affect on me and consequently my family throughout the years. He has literally influenced countless others, and I will tell you how.

I would describe Jack as one who sought for the virtue of self-mastery. How? Through his tireless energy and desire to sacrifice for the good of others by being a disciple of the greatest. There just aren't many who choose this path, especially with all the worldly success he enjoyed.

Jack Wheatley was born in a small farming community in southeast Idaho. The youngest of five, he learned to milk cows and drive a tractor—all at a very young age. After high school, he set his sights on West Point and was accepted. He thrived there because of the emphasis on leadership and discipline, which were things he was taught growing up.[7]

I remember attending missionary zone conferences with this man. He expected spit-shined shoes and old-fashioned starched collars. No one was really taught how to do this. You learned from your companion, and it was an acquired skill for sure. Some missionaries' collars had a crusty look due using too much corn starch. He might give a questioning look to those who appeared out of sorts. To be emissaries of Jesus, we needed to act the part, and this included being clean. Hopefully our hearts would shine through our young, inexperienced veneers.

President (that's what we called him) was never harsh or judgmental. Though he held the bar high, he saw the best in us and praised us legitimately. He expected us to think the best of ourselves and others who we served.

A mission was no finishing school. Some of the missionaries arrived in the field pretty raw or "green" as they say. Jack's training at West Point and time as the mayor of Palo Alto provided some needed culture. That didn't diminish, but only enhanced the drive and and sincerity of young men from the "sticks" (Wyoming or Idaho).

When he left the military, Jack went into commercial construction parlaying his training from the army corps of engineers. Partnering with one of his former employers, he went on to have a successful career in commercial construction. He also had great skill in planning, siting, and landscaping areas around those sights.

His children described their father as both frugal and generous. He was always other-focused. He taught his children to be aware of the needs that could be met through the efforts of philanthropy. He started a family foundation through which each child could choose a project to serve others. He instilled a motto in his children that he also tried to live by: "Weigh success not in gain, but in improvement of the world."

His greatest contribution over time may prove to be the Wheatley Institution, a program still growing. The Institution seeks creative and powerful ideas that will lead toward practical and constructive solutions to real societal issues. Its focus includes strengthening the family, improving education, pursuing international understanding and solutions, raising ethical standards, and defending moral values.[8]

While I was pursuing a doctorate in psychology, I was having trouble securing educational loans. I got up the nerve to write my former mission president for some money. He sent me a check for five thousand dollars, trusting I would use it for tuition and books. I will be ever grateful for his generosity and example.

Educational expenses are difficult to cover for students and their families in this era of high costs. It's a bit scary to incur a mountain of debt through student loans. I learned from a former missionary friend that Jack Wheatley, our mission president, had set aside a large sum of money for the children of all the missionaries who had served with him. The requirements were that the attend a Latter-day Saint college or university and with that, the Wheatley Scholarship would pay fifty percent of the tuition. It was an answer to prayer and a major relief to our family in helping us meet our children's educational expenses. I can't imagine the impact of helping hundreds if not thousands of students with their education expenses. What an impact he made.

Besides giving to Brigham Young University, Jack made substantial gifts to West Point, BYU–Idaho, Idaho State University, BYU–Hawaii,

Southern Virginia University, and the University of Utah, as well as Church history sites and temples for The Church of Jesus Christ of Latter-day Saints. "If you want to spread your good fortune," he said, "the best way to do it is to put it into young people. When you invest in their education . . . and they reinvest in the next person, and they reinvest—it's perpetual.

Maybe one of the truest displays of self-mastery is the willingness to sacrifice both time and money. The Wheatleys donated fifty percent of their annual income. He served as mayor of Palo Alto, served two missions with his wife, and hads been on and directed many boards, all in the quest to make the world a better place.

In explaining one of his great desires he said, "We're trying to develop people who feel that if there's a need, that they want to be a part of the solution." From my perspective, he's been doing this his entire life.

Many, if not most, who possess great wealth become self-indulgent. It would seem easy, even logical, to lavish oneself with the finer things of life; purchasing real estate, a yacht, an island, or numerous homes around the world. Not true of Jack and his wife Mary Lois. "I can't give it away fast enough," he has said, noting that he's always been blessed for his generosity. "I have been replenished every time I have given a large sum of money."

The pleasure of their lives has been to serve and see others benefit from their gifts. The Master said, "For whosoever will save his life shall lose it: and whosoever will lose his life for my sake shall find it." Working hard, sacrificing, and living generous has borne fruit, and will bear much more—in the lives of others for years to come, thanks to Jack Wheatley.[9]

What Are the Fruits of Self-mastery?

In sports, coaches often say there are no moral victories, that only wins count. When coaches say that, they are usually referring to a close, hard-fought game that still resulted in a loss. It may be that the other team had superior athletes, or that his own team fielded their less-than-best players, often because of injuries. At the end of the day in sports, it's about wins and losses. Few remember or are interested in the key plays or the drama of that day. It's always about wins and losses.

Contrary to sports, life is somewhat different. If we are winning battles in a war that rages on, those are wins. When you can manage your impulses and refrain from doing things that are harmful to yourself or others, that is a moral victory. And we ought to claim them. We don't win at everything nor can we be expected to. Losses or setbacks are part of the game of life and help us to prepare even better for the next battle. With more life experience and good coaching (mentoring), we will have more wins over time.

The game plan and plays drawn up, come from the moral principles we've been taught. They are fundamental and the ones that will help us gain yards as we move down the field. With practice we become more sound and play better. It's all in the execution.

Beyond the sports analogy, there will be a harvest of fruit when we model our lives after true, moral principles. As we do our best to follow them, they become easier. They may not get the attention of the world, but they do provide peace and a strengthened character. Some of these are:

- Being kind and compassionate;
- Releasing anger and forgiving;
- Giving thanks to God for one's blessings;
- Being loyal and faithful to loved ones;
- Respecting and honoring those who have sacrificed for us
- And so many more!

Trying to live a moral and integrity-filled life, will bring us treasures of the heart and mind—that surpass worldly understanding, and that results in confidence and joy.

Chapter 9

Courage

"Courage isn't having the strength to go on—it is going on when you don't have strength." —Napoleon Bonaparte

What Is Courage?

Courage has been described as having valor or being brave when faced with considerable challenges. Whatever the problem's source or degree of difficulty, courage impels one to face that challenge regardless of accompanying fear and uncertainty.

Think about your own life and the obstacles you've struggled with and overcome. Think of what you've learned about yourself when you chose to meet that hurdle head-on rather than sidestep it. I can recall times in my life when I chose the easy road and avoided the thing that would have built character.

The easy, convenient decision is not always best.

When I was in my late teens, I wanted to serve God by going on a mission for my church. I had planned on it while growing up. When I was eighteen, I met a young lady at college who I fell head over heels for. Falling is the first clue that things might be a bit unstable. We spent a lot of time with each other, and this grew into love. This was my first deeply felt (longer than a few dates) relationship. In the spring at the end of the school year, I formally began the process to receive an assignment as a missionary. Needless to say, I wasn't emotionally prepared at that point to go on a mission. I had made this woman my world; she had become my sole and soul interest.

I attempted to go on that mission(twice) unsuccessfully. When I entered the mission training center, I just couldn't concentrate on being a missionary. My heart wasn't in it. I was discouraged and felt I had let myself, others, and God down. The girl and I eventually broke up. My own angst was probably the biggest contributor for things falling apart between us.

I went back to school and finished my degree. Serving a mission never left my psyche. I wanted to try one more time, but I had anxiety, "What if I am not up to it? Maybe I'm just weak and can't do hard things." You know how we can be our own worst enemy. I made application one last time—to serve a mission. It probably didn't hurt that I was a little older, maybe a little more mature. It did help that I was emotionally ready and felt spiritually called to go. Many have been through far more difficult things, but for me it took some courage to follow my conscience and to care less about what others thought of my decision.

"Courage is the most important of all the virtues because without courage, you can't practice any other virtue consistently."[1]

What Will Challenge You from Being Courageous?

New experiences can create a sense of discomfort or uncertainty, even fear. Your first talk in front of a group of people; staying home alone overnight; the first day of your first "real" job; going to the hospital for surgery; these can all produce a sense of dread.

Sometimes the unknown can be likened to finding yourself shrouded in a thick fog. You look down the road without a clear path through. You wonder if you should slow down, stop, or even turn around and go back. There is so much unknown out there . . . so much fog . . . and you wonder what lies ahead.

When you get in your car and press the accelerator, you begin to see it's not so bad. The fog that looked so impenetrable is turning out to be increasingly transparent. As you move forward, you begin to see what you couldn't see before. Going from here to there has put you into another zone where things become clearer. But that didn't happen until you got into your car, put it into gear, and moved forward, if only carefully at first.

As you move along, the same thing happens again and again. Entering another zone, things clarify even more. You look at what is in front of you and around you, and you are now able to see street signs, landmarks, and buildings. There is relief for the time being. Now you have the information to make the decision of where you want to go.

Life is a lot like finding yourself in the fog. New experiences may seem paralyzing. But as you choose to move forward rather than remain stuck, your vision and perspective expand. Putting one foot in front of the other creates a sense of positive motion. Each new experience may be seen as an opportunity to take action. This increases your capability as you move from one zone to the next. This creates an awakening in yourself and the world around you.

Richie Norton says, "To escape fear, you have to go through it, not around."

Human beings are by nature finite and limited. And yet deep within each of us is the power to survive, overcome, and even succeed. Vince Lombardi believed that the difference between a successful person and others was not in their strength or knowledge but in a person's will. Do I want to ______? You fill in the blank.

Fear can be the greatest of illusions. If you think you can or can't, you're probably right.

"Courage is not the absence of fear, it's feeling the fear and facing it anyway"[2]

Believe in yourself and the process of life. Trust in other's sincere desire to help and in your ultimate ability to adapt to changing circumstances. You can and will succeed. You are made to do this! The fog is lifting, the landscape is clearer—it all starts with believing and that very important first step.

Many volunteers came from around the country (and the world) to the crowded NYC hospitals to help fight the often deadly COVID-19 virus of 2020. I came across a most interesting blog of a Utah nurse who reported her experiences each day. She began her account with what she learned—in her very first (brief) training before going onto the unit. The training leader quoted the inspiring but sobering words of Brene Brown:

"You can choose courage or comfort, you cannot have both."[3]

During her two-week stay, she encountered countless acts of courage from caregivers working extra-long shifts and risking their lives, in order to care for those fighting to live (another type of courage). Death became common.

She was forever changed from her own constant references of "it's legitimately war-like," and "this is modern war," recalling how patients were lined up one by one with no curtains. She poignantly described the emotional toll it had on a nurse, such as witnessing the pain of a family trying to get answers, or the agony of patients (knowing that they're dying) and laying there helpless.

One heartbreaking moment (and there were many), came when one of the nurse managers spotted her (the Utah nurse) in the hall and told her "our pregnant lady" had passed away. This visiting nurse already knew, but "realized this manager just needed to vent to someone about (this tragedy) it." Then she added, "I watched as this TOUGH, highly skilled ICU nurse lost it. It was like this one woman's death [finally] cracked her!" This is a kind of courage that few of us are ever called to bear.[4]

Desmond Doss was one of the most decorated veterans of World War II. Prior to his time in the service he led a relatively normal life. His mother raised him as a devout Seventh-day Adventist and instilled a Sabbath-keeping, nonviolent, and vegetarian lifestyle in him. He was clearly taught and lived by the strongest of moral principles.

As a young man, he was still living at home. Would his values carry him through the real world and in the heat of battle? (No pun intended.) Most of us have been taught correct principles and the difference between right and wrong. But do we know how we'll respond with the gritty issues, like in matters of life and death?

Before the war, Doss worked as a joiner in a shipyard. He signed with the military despite his strongly held beliefs about armed conflict. He refused to carry a weapon, so he became a medic. In boot camp, he was the target of ridicule because of his stance as a noncombatant. Imagine the irony of serving with men seeking the death of the enemy, with your own mission being to rescue and preserve life.

How would he respond in the line of fire when all hell broke loose? One of the strongest instincts for humans is to flee overwhelming danger, not entertain it by risking one's life.

Doss was serving in Okinawa when his unit was attacked on top of a cliff. Nearly every man was cut down. Doss, who was initially uninjured, made up a stretcher that could be lowered to the ground through a series of ropes and pulleys. All by himself and under enemy fire, he sought and found each soldier, then lowered them to safety. President Harry S. Truman presented him with the distinguished Medal of Honor, reporting to the assembled gathering that Doss had saved seventy-five men. Doss asserted it was closer to fifty.

This was only one instance of many where Doss demonstrated astonishing compassion and courage. His life story has been powerfully told in four different books and in the award-winning movie *Hacksaw Ridge*.

Near the time of the movie's release in an interview with his only son Desmond Doss Jr., he was asked why he thought his father did what he did. The younger Doss thought the movie answered this question best when it showed his father going back time and again to rescue another soldier and uttering the words, "Lord, just one more, help me get just one more."[5]

In the New Testament, Christ taught His disciples about the purest form of love:

"Greater love hath no man than this, that a man lay down his life for his friends."[6]

This is the highest form of courage.

After the war, Doss was unable to continue his work in carpentry due to his injuries. Soon after, he was also diagnosed with tuberculosis, which he contracted while serving in the Pacific. He ultimately lost a lung and five ribs. After an overdose of antibiotics, he was rendered completely deaf. He lived out his days managing a small farm in Georgia with his wife and son.

As a consolation, he was honored many times as a keynote speaker at gatherings to honor veterans. No doubt he inspired thousands, likely millions, with his moving example of selfless courage.

How to Find Courage in Your Life

More often than not, we need to find courage and fortitude in the seemingly small moments when we're faced with moral dilemmas. Will I stand up and speak out for what's right when the prevailing winds suggest otherwise? It's easier to slip out, duck down, or remain silent.

It takes integrity of the heart to be bold and fearless.

Think of Nathan Hale in the Revolutionary War when he was hung for spying. John Montresor, a British officer, offered him his tent so he could pen two final letters: one to his mother and the other to a brother officer. Hale was observed and recorded as "calm" and bearing a "gentle dignity," then shortly summoned to the gallows. He spoke only briefly with words never to be forgotten: "I only regret that I have but one life to lose for my country."[7]

It took great courage, for young Peter Buxtin, a twenty-seven-year-old social worker and epidemiologist, who was hired to interview patients with sexually transmitted diseases. During his work, he learned of the Tuskegee Experiment. This involved four hundred syphilitic participants, mostly poor sharecropper African American males, who had never been informed of their diagnosis or given medication for its treatment. The study's purpose was to observe the progression of syphilis at the expense of those who would suffer the ravages of the disease, including death. None of the men were ever offered penicillin which would have cured the disease. Mr. Buxtun, filled with righteous indignation, filed an official protest with the government on ethical grounds on two separate occasions—but to no avail. The government's response was that the study was not yet complete, and Buxton's concerns were irrelevant. Mr. Buxtun finally leaked information to the press, where it became a front headline in The New York Times. This ultimately led to a congressional hearing with the experiment being terminated.[8]

Courage is often manifest in simple, less dramatic ways, like someone resisting the peer pressure to indulge when everyone else is doing it.

I remember my daughter being dropped off very early at home after a prom dance at the local high school. She had gone with several couples in a group to the dance. Unbeknownst to her, the group had planned to leave early and return to one of the homes where the parents were gone, so they could party. This was a surprise to her. When we spoke about it, she was disappointed but had enough confidence in herself to kindly ask to be taken home. She obviously made no points with this group (which were some of the more popular kids), but she had found the courage to follow her conscience.

Demonstrating courage might be needed beyond what a situational crisis demands. It may be called upon when faced with a problem that is ongoing. It may require a series of decisions that come with increased difficulty. That's how it is sometimes. And the challenge that requires courage may come as your inner voice tells you, "This is your thing"; "You were called to do this"; "You can't walk away"; "If you don't own it, who will?"

The courage to take a stand is all about making a difference, by doing the right thing.

The following story describes another kind of courage. At the time I heard it, Dr. Foluso Fakorede was thirty-eight, built like a body builder; an African American cardiologist. Born in Nigeria and raised in New Jersey, he excelled in academics and graduated from medical school at Rutgers University. When things went south with his job in Tennessee, he looked even further south. With the suggestion of a friend who was from the area, he decided to visit the Mississippi Delta region. The area needed physicians and particularly black ones. It had some of the poorest people and highest rates of the medically underserved.

The area has a unique racial, cultural, and economic history. It is two hundred miles long and eighty-seven miles at its widest point. It was originally covered in hardwood forests, then developed as one of the richest cotton-growing areas in the nation prior to the Civil War. The region attracted speculators who developed the land along the river, which resulted in many becoming wealthy planters dependent on slave labor.

As Dr. Fakorede commenced his practice, he learned that the region (as well as other parts of the Deep South) had some of the highest amputations from diabetes of anywhere in the country. What was so alarming to him was that physicians were not routinely examining the patients' lower legs. Without arteriograms and other assessments, it wasn't possible to fully determine if revascularization (bringing blood flow around the blocked arteries in the leg), were possible, so as to prevent amputation.

He discovered a lack of interest among his peers to provide the kind of care these patients deserved. Other physicians were not applying best practice methods, and this infuriated Fakorede. With black patients losing limbs at a rate three times higher than other groups, he put up a billboard that read "Amputation Prevention Institute." Bottom line: the high rates of amputation seemed to be due to unequal access to health care, racist biases, and cuts in public health funding. Because of how the policies were written by hospitals, insurers, and the government, it was cheaper to amputate than do preventative care, which often lasted many years with diabetic patients.

It became nothing less than a crusade. Through hard work and sheer courage, Dr. Fakorede produced amazing results. In only two-years' time, he reduced major amputations from seventy-five to eighty-eight, a vast improvement. It's very difficult to move beyond the status quo and find better solutions to common problems. The patients in this region needed someone to champion their cause, someone who cared and possessed uncommon courage. So far, he's meeting that challenge.[9]

"A ship is safe in harbor, but that's not what ships are for."[10]

What Are the Fruits of Courage?

When we're brave enough to do the right thing at the right time, we'll feel we've been of some good. Is there anything better than the feeling that comes when you make a difference in someone's life? It's as if you were placed there, at that moment, for that very thing. You were fortunate enough to act and came through. I think the saying is "right on time."

Courage makes you feel alive. You don't have to save scores of men in a battle, or give your life for your country, or be the only person who will stand up and speak their conscience, but you might.

More often than not, it will be a number of things, small things, that no one will see but yourself and the One up above, that shows you are one who can be counted on, and that is a very beautiful thing!

The Virtues of Love

Gratitude, Forgiveness, Compassion

The virtues of love make earth life heavenly. They bring happiness, peace, and goodwill to all who practice them. The art of these virtues are evidence of the best gifts that humans can offer one another. When practiced, they demonstrate what a real progressive and ennobling society looks like. We participate in these virtues when we see each day as a blessing and see others as valuable, lovable, and unique human beings.

Chapter 10

Gratitude

"Gratitude unlocks the fullness of life. It turns what we have into enough, and more. It turns denial into acceptance, chaos to order, confusion to clarity. It can turn a meal into a feast, a house into a home, a stranger into a friend."
—Melody Beattie

What Is Gratitude?

Gratitude is the realization of one's many blessings. It is the sense of being loved and cared for. It's seeing the world through the eyes of abundance versus scarcity. It's knowing that you're God's child and that all of life is a gift—the good, as well as the hard and painful things. It's a level of understanding that all that has happened and will happen is part of a wonderful plan. It's the sense that everything will be ok in the larger scheme of things.

"Gratitude turns what we have into enough."[1]

I remember during Christmas one year (and I was an older adult at the time) I received a pair of wool slacks from my parents. I was in a room full of family, and we were opening gifts one at a time. After opening the box, I complained loudly how the pants were the wrong shade of gray, and the size wasn't right. I am now very embarrassed by my behavior. I was expressing the opposite of gratitude. What I did was awful, considering the kindness of t gesture. I wasn't focused on the gift or the gift giver but my own gratification. Gratitude is our projection and nearly always about our perceptions and perspectives.

"Gratitude will shift you to a higher frequency, and you will attract much better things."[2]

I have learned a lot about gratitude from others. It's not that I've been ungrateful, though I've had my share of the many good things of life. Most of the time, many of us don't fully realize our blessings. It's interesting that it takes being down and to be without to value what it's like to be "up" and realize how good life can be. Then again, gratitude isn't always about material things.

I went through a difficult time in my life when I was diagnosed with a life-threatening illness. I was humbled, then grateful, when my health started to improve. It seems that we all need is to experience contrasts. We don't seem to fully appreciate our life, our health, or any number of other blessings until we lose them.

What Interferes with Finding Gratitude?

I think I lost an opportunity to feel and offer gratitude, as shown in the example when I received the Christmas gift.

Cynicism, entitlement, greed, and selfishness are the killers of gratitude. The world has these in abundance; thus, it takes effort to look up, to look the other way, and take the road less traveled.

Isn't all of life a gift if we'll look at it that way? And that is precisely what gratitude and a thankful heart is all about. Now that I am getting older (past sixty), life has become more precious, more valued, and probably a little less certain. Our physical bodies, this temporal existence, won't last forever as we know it.

I'm reminded of the movie *Awakenings* starring Robert De Niro and Robin Williams. In it, Leonard Lowe, played by Robert De Niro, and other psychiatric patients are living in an institution with catatonia, a form of schizophrenia that renders them nonfunctional. One by one they are administered the drug L-dopa, and they begin to experience a miraculous awakening. Through slow improvement (cognitively and emotionally), they begin to reclaim their former selves.

Dr. Malcolm Sayer (played by Robin Williams), receives a call late one night from Leonard, who is having his own profound awakening. He excitedly asks Dr. Sayer to return to the hospital, explaining that some important things have happened, and he must talk now. When they meet up at the office, Leonard launches into his discovery:

> Leonard: "We've got to tell everyone; we've got to remind them . . . how good it is!"

> Dr. Sayer: "How good what is, Leonard?"

> Leonard: "People have forgotten what life is all about, they've forgotten what it is like to be alive, to be reminded of what they have . . . and what they can lose . . . to feel the joy of life, the gift of life, the freedom of life, the wonderment of life!"

Later, Dr. Sayer addresses his colleagues regarding Leonard's dramatic change and the impact this has had on him (Dr. Sayer). With the drug' effects only temporary, and patients reverting to their original catatonic states, he describes how all of this has led to an awakening of his own. He explains, "As the chemical window closed, another wakening took place . . . that the human spirit is more powerful than any drug and that's what needs to be nurtured . . . work, play, friendship, family; these are the things that matter. These are the things we've forgotten . . . the simplest things!"[3]

Sometimes we may have our own dramatic experience that brings home the realization of how great life is. Other times, it's more often the gentle, subtle messages of the wonder and splendor of it all. They're usually the simplest of things.

For me, it's the coolness and freshness of the morning air and how a perfectly new day is mine once again; it is going barefoot into the backyard to pick fresh raspberries for breakfast; it is meeting together at the family cabin and catching up on all the news of everyone's family; it's seeing your children grow into adults and beginning to thrive and be happy as you always hoped and prayed for; it' feeling and sharing love for those you care about; it's realizing God is good, and that He's here with you and me!

What else is there really?

Look for the beauty all around you. Sure, we'll forget all of this and have bad moments and difficult days. But the goodness and meaning of life is always there, if we choose to be mindful and grateful.

How to Foster Gratitude

I worked in a hospital for a number of years and visited patients daily. It was such an incredible experience to converse with others who had been through some extremely hard times. There was a blind person; another who had to be in dialysis many hours each day; a person who was unable to read and could barely write; others on the verge of "passing over" from the ravages of cancer; those with lost limbs; and those who lived with chronic debilitating illnesses. These are just a few examples of the conditions I found in patients I visited.

As I listened to them talk of their experience day after day (usually unsolicited), many would begin to speak from a place of gratitude. They would express a lot of thankfulness and appreciation. It was an amazing spiritual experience to witness. Hopefully at one time or another we've all experienced talking with sick people who share from a place of thanksgiving. These special people, with their lives shattered, so to speak, were teaching others (me) how to be grateful and find joy when all hell breaks loose in your life.

Gratitude is truly a gift that can be sought for and received, a gift many acquire through the chiseling process of many difficult, painful days.

I was always astonished when patients, the ones hurting and scared, would go out of their way to express appreciation for the care they were receiving. They sometimes mentioned the specific name of a nurse or housekeeper who had waited on them. Of course, there are several factors that might affect a patient's openness and willingness to share. It may be their level of pain, how medicated they were, whether they liked to converse, their personality, or perhaps just timing.

But when someone who has been newly diagnosed with cancer, or recently had a limb amputated, or is in the midst of serious pain tells you how much they feel cared for or appreciated, it really takes your breath away. You see, some folks have developed and honed the gift of gratitude. They have learned to see what is right with their life, and all that is going on around them. They realize that life is a gift and that every day, maybe every moment, is an opportunity to give thanks and make someone else's day a little better, in spite of their own distress.

Here are a few of their stories:

I remember one woman who was hospitalized frequently with a chronic condition. When I inquired of the quality of the care she received, she simply said, "I feel loved here, the nurses are kind to me!"

There was a man with terminal cancer who possessed great faith. Nothing more medically could be done for him. The doctors even told him how many days he had to live (based on science). He wanted to know, and it proved to be a good thing in his case—he died on the very day they predicted. And the good thing was he wasn't in any pain. He was surrounded in those last days by his wife, children, and occasional visits from grandchildren. I met many of them. I asked what we could do for him. He said, "Sing to me, I'd love to hear my favorite hymns and cowboy songs." It was truly a sight to behold. We gathered around his bed, about eight or ten of us in the room (nurses, managers, clerks, secretaries). As we sang, there was not a dry eye. During the last days that we visited, he was always expressing gratitude to God, his life, his family (he loved his grandkids), and the nursing staff. When I returned to work the following Monday, I checked to see if he'd made it; and been taken down to our extended care facility. He hadn't and had passed peacefully as predicted earlier that morning. I will never forget him and his grateful heart!

I remember meeting a blind man during my daily rounds in the hospital. He was being treated for some other serious ailments. He was a single parent, overwhelmed with the care of children, and struggling economically. He was, however, very grateful for his care and caregivers. He said everyone was treating him with kindness. He explained that one of his biggest challenges in life was having little to do that felt personally meaningful. I learned that he played music by ear through just listening to songs. He had no formal training. For some time, we'd been looking for a musician who could play in one of the waiting rooms of the hospital. Bingo, the light came on, and I made the invitation: "We [the hospital] have a proposal for you. Would you be willing to come and play for us? We will provide you with transportation, an electronic keyboard, and free lunch." I explained that he would be a volunteer, and that his services would be valued and greatly appreciated. I further suggested he mull it over and decide if it was right for him. I contacted him a few days later. He agreed to do it and was grateful for the invitation. He said it was an answer to prayers.

A serious but not uncommon problem associated with diabetes is the loss of a toe or foot and sometimes a limb. I became associated with a middle-aged gentleman who had lost his leg. Over the next few years, he returned to the hospital many times. There was a need for additional surgeries and treatment. Though I saw him during very difficult times of pain and anguish, he was almost always in an upbeat mood and positive about the care he'd received. He seemed to grow from the things that he suffered. What was so remarkable was his thankfulness for the efforts of others treating him like a person (not an amputee) and for the little but good things in his life.

On another occasion, I became acquainted with a patient in the ICU of the hospital. He was very ill and impoverished. He had no insurance coverage and no way to pay for his inpatient stay or for the outpatient treatment that would be needed as a follow-up to maintain his health. Social Services visited him and left him the paperwork required for state assistance. He likely would qualify. Several days later when the social worker checked back, nothing had been done. He was encouraged to get going. Everyone felt he was well enough to work on it as he sat each day in a chair watching TV. Eventually, he was kindly but directly asked what was the matter. Why would he not help himself by filling out the papers? He answered haltingly that he could barely read and write and was embarrassed to ask for help. Several of the staff jumped in and helped him complete the forms. He was sincerely surprised at all those who wanted to help him. He was humbled and very appreciative. He said that this wouldn't have happened at the other places he'd been. He was truly grateful; you could see it in his countenance and outward demeanor.

Each time I witnessed these and other similar experiences, I found myself thinking, "Wow, I haven't been through all of this or that, and I complain about my life, and I don't give thanks nearly enough."

Try opening your heart and mind a little more as you observe others and listen for the voice of gratitude. It's present more than you think. It's incredible how many of us don't practice this virtue enough.

This great gift of life, the ability to savor each day with all its blessings, is ours for the choosing.

Here's one last story. This is about a woman in the extended care unit of the hospital. She was confined to a wheelchair and very much wanted to walk again. "I want to be normal and get out of here," she often would say to me.

I remember too that she often expressed gratitude—gratitude for the caregivers and the many friends she'd made there. She purposely sat in a location where she could come in contact with many of the residents and visitors. As people passed by, she would initiate a conversation and offer encouraging words. She would ask some to come closer, so she could place a happy-face sticker on their clothing. She expressed her gratitude by reaching out to others. What she did made a difference.

I got to know this woman a little more than some of the others. We became friends. When I was in the unit, I would briefly stop and visit to try and lift her spirits. At the time, my wife and I were having some trouble with one of our adult children, and she picked up on my distress. She asked me to tell her a little more. She listened intently, and then with some confidence said "Your son's going to be ok, he just needs a little more time to grow up and realize who he is."

In my simple attempt to encourage her, the tables had turned, and she was helping me. This woman tucked away in a nursing home was, on the surface, emotionally fragile and often in need of counsel and support. But that day, she was the one doing the lifting. By being sensitive and really listening, she offered hope and helped another (me) to feel very grateful! I thanked her warmly.

You might wonder why I share so many stories. I share them because they are true and come from real people who were suffering. Suffering from chronic conditions many of us may never experience. We learn best by telling and hearing stories. We too can be grateful in spite of the challenges that life hands us.

All these folks were inspiring to me. They not only learned to endure life's hard things but to endure them well. Buddha said it cleverly with the following words:

"Let us rise up and be thankful, for if we didn't learn a lot today, at least we learned a little, and if we didn't learn a little, at least we didn't get sick, and if we got sick at least we didn't die; so, let us all be thankful."[4]

As has been said, "We do survive every moment, after all, except the last one!"[5]

Might as well be grateful!

What Are the Fruits of Gratitude?

I believe I'm now a little more aware of the blessings that flow to us in various forms each day. These blessings present themselves as daily opportunities for gratitude. Gratitude doesn't change reality, only our perception of it, but it transforms it in a positive way.

If you want to feel more gratitude, express more gratitude. Do it in a journal, and express it freely as often as you can. This will build a reservoir of thankfulness within. It will increase your awareness and understanding of life's abundance, a sense of peace, and a compassion for others.

And that makes all the difference in the world.

Chapter 11

Forgiveness

"Forgiveness is not always easy. At times, it feels more painful than the wound we suffered, to forgive the one that inflicted it. And yet, there is no peace without forgiveness." —Marianne Williamson

What Is Forgiveness?

Forgiveness has been defined by the psychology profession as a "conscious, deliberate decision to release feelings of resentment or vengeance toward a person or group who has harmed you, regardless of whether they actually deserve your forgiveness."[1]

"Forgiveness is an act of the will, and the will can function regardless of the temperature of the heart."[2]

"Forgiveness is like faith. You have to keep reviving it."[3]

Forgiveness is wiping the slate clean, so we can create a new message. We forgive to set each other free. Forgiveness is a gift that is both given and received, so that both may become the beneficiaries.

"We must develop and maintain the capacity to forgive. He who is devoid of the power to forgive is devoid of the power to love. There is some good in the worst of us and some evil in the best of us. When we discover this, we are less prone to hate our enemies."[4]

What Will Make Forgiveness Difficult?

I remember one of the most common issues people presented in therapy was the difficulty they had in forgiving. They had trouble letting go of what happened to them. They struggled to find the focus to live in the present. I knew the moment they began moving forward with their life by their language. They stopped talking about the things that they hated or had hurt them. They started investing in their personal plans and projects. Their minds were clearer, they were happier in the present with new ideas for the future. They were a new creature.

Of course, there's a laundry list of things that people may despise. And indeed, some of those things are mighty big.

Any significant loss or change leads to pain and stress. And then this is followed with an adjustment period. Some of these things will take time to process, sometimes a lot of it. When you have invested so much energy and attention into a person or thing, there is a strong connection, there is feeling and love. When you take away what someone has loved or invested in, it's going to hurt. It can feel like a death. They will need to mourn if they are to heal.

And they will usually never forget it. Deep loss leaves a mark, an impression, maybe a scar. When others describe that "forgiving is forgetting," it is somewhat of a misnomer. We can definitely forgive, but in doing so we are changed forever inside! The forgetting (if there has been forgiveness) is actually the lessening of pain. There is still the memory most of the time for most people.

Does a veteran who has experienced the violence of war ever really forget what he's been through?

Will a child who went to bed hungry at night erase that experience from their memory?

Can a woman who was cheated on by the man that she loved ever trust him again?

Can an adult who was constantly yelled at as a child until they left home let go of those feelings?

There are many factors that influence the art of forgiving. Some make a better go of it than others. It is clearly possible to heal and move forward. Maybe the ones who struggle the most are the ones who seemingly escaped for a time but are drawn back in by that same pain, only with different places and people.

People forgive in their own way and time. Some won't due to the severity of the damage or because of their own choice. I have found that forgiveness for many is a kind of redepositing or relocating. Memory banks are never entirely shut off but can be muted. If someone has never experienced a caring, loving relationship but wants one and finds it, it can do wonders in the reprogramming of their life and memories. Our minds and souls have plasticity. They can be reworked like clay.

C. S. Lewis was one of the most influential Christian authors of the last century. He admitted having many attempts to forgive someone who had been cruel to him. He struggled to let it go. He even prayed for this man, because he knew Jesus wanted him to. He related,

> Last week while at prayer, I suddenly discovered—or felt as if I did—that I had really forgiven someone I have been trying to forgive for over thirty years. Trying, and praying that I might. When the thing actually happened (sudden as the longed-for cessation of one's neighbor's radio), my feeling was, but it's so easy, why didn't I do it ages ago?

Lewis made it clear that his ability to forgive was not of his own doing. He reflected, "A discord has been resolved and it is certainly the great Resolver who has done it."[5]

Why Should We Forgive?

The story is told of my great-great-grandfather Joseph Albert Harris, who became disgruntled when he didn't receive a promised promotion from the company he worked for. (It's kind of sketchy, and we don't have great detail, but it's what's been handed down.) He was so upset that he turned away from his religious beliefs and began drinking. What other things may have contributed to the downward spiral of his life is uncertain, but the next three generations were of lives filled with the abuse of tobacco and alcohol and probably more. It was said that he was angry and never forgave what "they" did to him. "They" was the business he worked for, and it was owned by the church he was a part of.

When my father was born, he was quite unaware of his rich spiritual heritage. He did not like the lifestyle of using substances and chose a healthier path filled with moderation and spirituality. Important decisions can have profound effects and can change the course of the next generation. Just as my grandfather's choices took others away, my father's decision brought others back. In turning to God, my father reaped wonderful blessings for himself and his family.

The moral of this story is to not get stuck, and don't stay angry. Gather yourself up, forgive and move on. Besides yourself, you never know how your decisions will affect others.

"Forgive yourself for your faults and mistakes and move on."[6]

No one knows precisely why it can take many months or years to forgive. Perhaps it's based on our level of sincerity, effort expended, or other spiritual and psychological processes at play.

Sometimes it's only through the passage of time and a deeper understanding of the past, coupled with positive life experiences that we find the ability to put things into perspective. We discover that we now have some control, and we can avoid future victimizations. We can stand up, lean in, and push back.

A remarkable thing that really helps is to actually say the words "I forgive," "I let go" or "I choose to move on." One can do this by looking into a mirror while reciting those words, through symbolic letter writing or journaling, or simply telling the person face-to-face. It's important if you choose the latter to not be looking for a certain kind of response from the other person, such as, "Oh, thank you so much, I have been waiting for this all of my life!"

When you finally truly forgive, it will cleanse you, and you'll be ready to move forward. It's because you've already done the internal work, the processing, mulling it around,and working it through like kneading dough. When you forgive, you really do change the world. That's because you've become different and feel different. It will change how you see and treat others and (maybe) most importantly yourself. Forgiveness is truly a virtue, a spiritual gift that keeps on giving.

Many in the field of mental health (and now it is documented scientifically) believe there is an association between physical illness and the mind, which is where our thoughts, memories, and emotions originate. I used to do a visualization with clients where this idea was manifest in the following phrase:

If you hold on with your mind, you hold on with your body, and if you hold on with your body, you hold on with your mind.

There are many examples that can be given in this regard. We know that the immune system is influenced by stress hormones, and these same hormones are activated by the perceptions of our life experiences at any given time.

Think of an experience when you were fearful. Was there a change in your heart rate or blood pressure? Did you sweat, have dry mouth, or need to use the bathroom more? Recall a time you experienced significant anger or stress during the day, only to go to bed that night and be unable to asleep. Imagine if you were caught up in these emotional and physical states for prolonged periods of time. For some, even many, this is a reality. On one cable station, there are literally recurring, nonstop ads for sleep and pain relief on a nightly basis.

These emotional states may come from a myriad of situations: a boss who uses threats or other forms of intimidation; chronic poverty, which usually affects one's nutrition, housing, and health care, and can rob one from the hope of a better day; or a very unhappy relationship that doesn't seem fixable. Can you see how illness and disease begins in the perceptions and processes of the mind? Our mind, body, and spirit are not mechanistic but synergistic, thoroughly connected as a whole.

Sometimes we may need to separate ourselves from certain people or environs in order to improve our lives. That's a structural change. It may be what is best and necessary.

Sometimes the needed change is what we carry around in our mind and heart. It's less about the physical environment and more about the internal one. When we learn how, then choose to forgive, we can literally improve our health, sometimes in remarkable ways.

Not long ago, I read a fascinating story of a woman who "wanted to be become a prosecutor so she could lock up child molesters."[7] Having suffered sexual abuse at the hands of her own father, hers was a tortuous journey to find herself, yet it ultimately led to her life's work. Her name: Sujatha Baliga.

Baliga was born and raised in Pennsylvania, the youngest child of Indian immigrants. As a result of the abuse, she dyed her hair blue and cut herself. She loathed herself and felt like an outcast at her mostly white school. As a young teen, she had a growing realization she was not the cause of her problems, but they were due to her father who had done terrible things to her. He died two years later of a heart attack.

She found that she excelled in school and as an undergrad at Harvard–Radcliffe, it became clear to her of her life's mission. After college, she went to New York to work with battered women. With law school imminent, she followed her boyfriend to Mumbai when he won a fellowship to start school there. While in India, she had a total breakdown even though she'd been receiving therapy for a while. She described feeling: "Oh, my God, I've got to fix myself before I start law school."

The next series of events proved to be fortuitous and life-changing. She felt inspired to take a train to Dharamsala (in the Himalayas), which was home to a large Tibetan exile community. She heard these Tibetans tell horrific stories of times when they were in the hands of the Chinese army. There was rape, even children being made to kill their parents. Really awful things. She wondered how these people could go on and be smiling, even happy again. They answered her, "By forgiving!"

Baliga was staying at a guesthouse and learned from the family operating it that people often wrote to the Dalai Lama (the 1989 Nobel Peace Prize winner who lived in the community) for advice. They suggested she try it. Baliga wrote to him, "Anger is killing me, but it motivates my work. How do you work on behalf of oppressed and abused people without anger as the motivating force?"

As she dropped the letter off at the Dalai Lama's front gate, she was told to return in about a week. Later, when arriving back, she expected only a written response; she was instead invited in to meet with the Dalai Lama for an hour.

He recommended she do two things: meditate which she agreed to do, and "to align herself with the enemy and consider opening her heart to them."

She explained with laughter to his latter advice, "I'm going to school to lock those [bad] guys up."

His response, as he patted her on the knee, "Okay, just meditate!"

Baliga returned to the US and enrolled in a ten-day course on meditation. On the tenth and final day, she described an unexpected experience that brought relief and a complete forgiveness of her father. She described it as having "a complete relinquishment of hatred, anger, and the desire for revenge and retribution."

After finishing law school, she clerked for a federal judge, and it was there that she learned of a movement know as restorative justice. This would further change her life. Not only had she changed her own life for the better but she was now involved in a process of helping others find forgiveness and reconciliation, as well as a more personalized plan of justice. Restorative justice attempts to understand and assist in the needs of the various parties touched by a specific crime (e.g., perpetrator, victim, family members, the courts, etc.).[8]

I think Baliga's story illustrates an important principle. It's pretty clear she was looking for answers. This desire led her to finding a clear resolution to her problem. She went into therapy, traveled, listened to her heart, then found herself sitting with one of the world's great spiritual leaders to receive wise counsel. Some might call this the hand of God or the doings of a compassionate universe. If you look at your life, you may realize you've been influenced by some great force too in fulfilling the desires of your heart.

I have found that when someone desires change (or anything), and it is strong enough, they are granted in finding a way that brings things to fruition. We might call this the fruits of will and intention, which in this case led to receiving forgiveness. She sought the gift, did the work, and then was enabled by others with their knowledge and experience.

Most of us will never forget the tragic incident that occurred near Lancaster, PA., in the fall of 2006.

A thirty-two-year-old milk truck driver known to the community (and who likely knew some of the children) walked into the local Amish school and shot ten girls between the ages of nine and thirteen. The shooter was Charles Roberts, described by his wife as a really good family man with no previous criminal record. Troubled by pathological guilt and depression, he planned and carried out this gruesome attack, then committed suicide. A grandfather of one of the murdered Amish girls said on the very day of her death: "We must not think evil of this man."

In the midst of their own shock and grief, the Amish community didn't cast blame. They reached out with remarkable grace and compassion toward the killer's family. In fact, that very day, Amish neighbors visited the Roberts family to comfort them in their sorrow and pain. Surprisingly, they outnumbered the non-Amish at Roberts's funeral.[9]

What Are the Fruits of Forgiveness?

Why should we forgive? Because without forgiveness, we will continue to suffer. When we are suffering, others are also affected by our grief and suffering; and that contributes to more suffering. Just as compassion begets more compassion, suffering does the same.

"The only way out of the labyrinth of suffering is to forgive."[10]

Think of the power of the act of forgiving. It can heal a friendship, save a marriage, even make heaven possible to one who believes.

Abraham Lincoln at the Civil War's end could have acted on the practice, "to the victor goes the spoils." But that would have been unjust. Instead, he took the high road that was necessary for forgiveness, and he *acted*, "With malice toward none, with charity for all . . . to finish the work we are in, to bind up the nation's wound . . . to do all which may achieve and cherish a just and lasting peace."[11]

Thus, the fruits of forgiveness bring a sense of healing, joy, and peace.

Chapter 12

Compassion

"Too often we underestimate the power of a touch, a smile, a kind word, a listening ear, an honest compliment, or the smallest act of caring, all of which have the potential to turn a life around." —Leo Buscaglia

What Is Compassion?

Compassion is a special kind of love or benevolence. It is the recognition of, and effort made, to relieve suffering. In its purest sense, it means "to suffer together."

When we have empathy for others, we cannot look away or refrain from helping.

I will depart somewhat from the truest meaning of compassion in these writings; all of us are suffering in some way. The difference is only the kind and degree. Suffering is as much mental and emotional as it is physical. Thus, the descriptions and stories shared will be about any kind of genuine care or concern.

One of the best-known parables as told by Jesus in the New Testament is of that of the good Samaritan. When a lawyer asked the Master what he needed to do to inherit eternal life, He responded, "Thou shalt love the Lord thy God with all thy heart, and with all thy soul, and with all thy mind . . . (and to) love thy neighbour as thyself" (Luke 10:27).

He then described how a certain man traveling to Jericho fell among thieves, was robbed, beaten, and left for dead. Both a priest and Levite (religious men of the day) passed by. But a certain Samaritan (scorned by the Jews of the day) as he journeyed came to the man and had compassion on him.

And went to him, and bound up his wounds, pouring in oil and wine, and set him on his own beast, and brought him to an inn, and took care of him. And on the morrow when he departed, he took out two pence, and gave them to the host, and said unto him, Take care of him; and whatsoever thou spendest more, when I come again, I will repay thee.[1]

What Interferes with Being Compassionate?

Like many of the other virtues, we sometimes, even often, dismiss the impulses to take the time to help. These moments to act are often brief and dissipate quickly. I have passed someone a thousand times who is broken down along the road, telling myself, "I have to get to work, someone else can stop and help them."

There are clearly other opportunities to do good with so much suffering, and they come in all degrees. There are homeless shelters, lonely neighbors, family members who need our minds and hearts.

We don't think we'll be good at compassion or are up to the task. Someone else is kinder, better at listening, etc.

We may be afraid of rejection.

The big thing is taking the time to show that we care. It's the effort, the gesture of choosing to get involved, and trying to make a difference that matters.

There was a large sociological study conducted in the US a number of years ago. It was an investigation into learning whether people have adequate resources or connectivity to others, particularly when they're needing help. People were asked this specific question: "How many people do you have in your life that you feel close enough to share a personal problem?"

When the question was asked in 1996, the most common response was three people. In 2004, the answer was one, and twenty-five percent of that group indicated they had no one to talk to. That is sobering. That's a lot of people that are hurting and likely wanting and needing a friend.[2]

"Be kind, for everyone you meet is fighting a harder battle."[3]

How to Be and Act More Compassionate

We can show kindness in countless ways each day. It need not be a high and mighty thing. The greatest impact we will have will probably be with our families, neighbors, and communities, and maybe where we work. A smile, a helping hand, giving a ride, babysitting—all gestures of caring. Sometimes we can do much good in other places in the world, but we ought to look for the needs of others that are right in front of us.

In the pandemic of 2020, a group of health care workers volunteered their services by traveling to NYC to work in the hospitals. They were coming from a state with a relatively low rate of infection. They did this because they wanted to make a difference. Their brothers and sisters needed help; thus, they saw a need and wished to fill it.

One of the nurses from the group explained how difficult it was to witness so much death. She described how she and others would pray for the patient's family (as they couldn't be there), and then how they would hold the patient's hand as they passed on. She described that they created handmade cards for the surviving family and include a finger print of the family's loved one, as well as an EKG strip (heart strip) to give the, so they would have something to remember them by.

This same caregiver described seeing patients lined up one by one with no curtains, (She had never seen this before.) She described the nurses becoming "burned out" and how it was showing because of all the stress. She further related that when patients had pictures of their families with them in the room, it helped them a great deal. She added that it helped the staff to see their patients as human beings—someone's mother or father, brother or sister, son or daughter. She explained how these patients deserved the utmost care.[4]

"Compassion is the basis of morality."[5]

I was touched by a headline in the news recently. Because I live in the Intermountain West, I follow the Utah Jazz, an NBA basketball team. I must confess it's easier to follow a team when they're competitive. The Jazz were in two NBA finals two years in a row with the Chicago Bulls ('97, '98). Michael Jordan, playing with the Bulls, was the Jazz's nemesis;

he was everyone's nemesis. Karl Malone was the leading scorer and most popular player for the Jazz at the time. He said recently,

> Me and Stockton have been talking a lot. Our coach [Jerry Sloan] is not doing well [with Parkinson's disease]. I want you guys [other retired NBA players] to pray for Coach Sloan. It's a small fraternity, I want to tell each of you . . . if you guys ever need me, I'm there, drop of a hat. I am just a phone call away. You made me the player that I am. I'm grateful for you guys.[6]

Sloan died four days later.

Now, what Malone did was a rather simple thing. Many of us feel gratitude and compassion for family and friends, particularly in their hour of need. What I appreciated most about Malone was he wasn't afraid to share true feelings in the public square. Maybe not the hardest thing to do, but it's becoming rarer, and he did it with sincerity. We can all show a little more compassion when we feel it or have our heartstrings pulled.

It's been reported that there is a multiplication of loving energy when someone does a kind or caring act. Studies indicate when you offer compassion in any capacity, several amazing things take place. The helper and the helped actually benefit a third party: the observer. This is a time when 1+1=3. Of course, the helper feels inspired and lifted by serving the helped person; the helped person feels someone cares; and in a somewhat surprising twist, the observer, the one watching it all unfold, is inspired as well. Scientists say that even a brief exposure to others doing good elevates our mood and motivates us to act unselfishly.[7]

This gives fresh meaning to the adage "one good turn deserves another" or put in a more contemporary way, "pay it forward!" There is really a natural high in serving, which is another form of compassion.

Compassion is contagious!

Recently, my father and I were visiting a restaurant. It was one where you walked down the line as they assemble your food on the other side of the counter. There were people in front and behind me, and we were all trying to practice social distancing. As I made my way to the register to pay for our food, the clerk explained, "Oh, you won't need to pay, the person ahead of you just picked up your tab." What I experienced surprised me, having never been part of something quite like this.

Just as the person ahead of me paid my bill, so too was his meal paid for by the person in front of him. Because I was touched by this kindly gesture, I felt inspired to pay for the guy following me. I don't know how long this chain may have continued.

In effect, everyone still had a bill, and no one got a free lunch. The bigger lesson for me was that a stranger could go out of his or her way and do a nice thing simply because they wanted to, and that this event inspired others to do similar acts of kindness. I already knew this but was still impressed in experiencing it.

An important side note: the fellow who started it all (the one who was two people ahead of me) was a tall, rather large Native American. I remember that, for whatever reason, he bothered me. He had his mask down and he was moving slow and talking constantly to the food clerk. I was judging him negatively in a number of ways. When I realized the beautiful thing he had done, I was humbled. I think many of us judge a book by its cover. I did and was wrong! I couldn't possibly see his heart and what he was about to do.

My wife and I were having some problems with a big box home improvement store. We had purchased a new front door and were informed that the products were available and only needed to ship from the warehouse. Six weeks later, everything was still on back order. I was paying interest on a product I never received. There was little if any communication from the store; each time it was us who initiated contact. Though certainly not close to a really big thing, we were letting it bother us. My wife was angrier than I'd seen her in a while. When we went to Lowe's, we were directed to an installation person. She was nice but felt we needed to talk to her manager. The manager sincerely listened and was apologetic. When he learned the details, he reduced our bill by about one hundred dollars. Besides offering great customer service, he recognized we were unhappy and tried to alleviate it. We've all been told many times in retail situations, "I'm sorry, I can't help you." In these instances, besides getting little help, you don't even feel heard. This is an instance that truly made a difference and lifted our spirits. We spoke about it for the next few days.

What compassion does is it offers comfort to the individual, right there, right then. What may not be seen is that someone's belief in humanity is strengthened or restored. My wife and I were both a little happier, more buoyant. And it wasn't just the money. In the period of time in which we live, with the pandemic and social unrest, we'd like to feel someone out there still cares, even if through small gestures. That's priceless!

A few years ago, I became acquainted with a woman who had a pretty incredible story. Looking back, I realized meeting her was no accident. How I learned about her story was nearly as remarkable as the story itself. It started with my participation in an initiative to put up the portraits of medical pioneers on the walls in various parts of our hospital. We referred to these humanitarians, these innovators, as "healing heroes." The purpose of this effort was to remind caregivers of the importance that compassion plays in the healing of a patient. We thought that if they could see these leaders, it might inspire them in the work they were also doing to help others.

We believed at the hospital that all employees were caregivers, especially as they chose to be compassionate and fulfill the other parts of their job description. We adopted a key principle known as the Mother Test. The Mother Test, simply put, was to treat patients (and one another) as if they were your own mother. This of course was both a challenge and an opportunity. What many of us learned was that you can demonstrate competence in your job skills and still be compassionate. The two ideas were not mutually exclusive.

Back to my story. It took us a few days to strategically place the portraits around the hospital. It was only a few weeks later that Todd (our advisor from the Erie Chapman Foundation) came for a site visit regarding our progress in qualifying for certification as a healing hospital. He was here to mentor and assist us in teaching our employees how to be ever compassionate as they fulfilled work responsibilities.

As Todd and I stopped to discuss one of the portraits, which was of Mother Teresa, a woman passing behind us exclaimed, "I knew that woman!" Needless to say, we were surprised and turned to engage her. Her name was Marilyn Slade. She briefly described that she had been a Christian missionary in southern California some years earlier. She became very sick, and some had suggested that she go and seek help at the Scripps Hospital in La Jolla, California. Mother Teresa just happened to also be staying in the same hospital. She had been doing charity work in Tijuana just across the border from San Diego and had fallen ill with pneumonia and congestive heart failure.

During her stay at Scripps, Marilyn was feeling well enough that one day she stepped outside her room. Looking up, she saw a group of people (Mother Teresa's entourage) motioning to her. She found her way to their place in the hospital, then learned that Mother Teresa desired to give her a blessing. Marilyn was told that Mother Teresa had seen a beautiful aura about her and wanted to give her a blessing. In the blessing, Marilyn was promised that her health would improve, that she had a work to do, and would not be taken before her time.

"If we have no peace, it is because we have forgotten that we belong to each other."[8]

Meeting Marilyn would not have occurred if Todd and I had not been conversing in front of Mother Teresa's portrait at the very moment that Marilyn walked by. Marilyn might have stopped and reminisced of her experience with this grand lady, but we would never have met.

There were several layers of love here, such as the beautiful story, having a local connection to Mother Teresa who was one of the great healers of our time, making friends with Marilyn—a wonderful human being, and the serendipitous timing when we all met. This is what is referred to by some as a tender mercy from above—another kind of compassion.

Karen Armstrong is a British author, commentator, and visionary who has devoted her life to championing peace and a more compassionate world. At the age of eighteen, she entered the convent and became a member of the Sisters of the Holy Child Jesus. Having suffered both physical and psychological abuse there, she left the convent after seven years. With an Oxford education in English, she turned to a career in writing and in research on comparative religion. In her quest to increase compassion worldwide, she has addressed members of the US Congress, lectured policy makers at the US State department and Council on Foreign Relations, and leaders of Muslim countries. She is currently an ambassador for the UN Alliance of Civilizations.

Her heart's desire has been to assemble a movement around that which the world's religious leaders could work together for peace and understanding. Called the Charter for Compassion, it was brought to fruition in 2009. She has stated,

> I believe that religion isn't [just] about believing things. It's about what you do. It's ethical alchemy. It's about behaving in a way that changes you, that gives you intimations of holiness and sacredness . . . We urgently need to make *compassion* a clear, luminous and dynamic force in our polarized world. Rooted in a principled determination to transcend *selfishness,* compassion can break down political, dogmatic, ideological, and religious boundaries. Born of our deep interdependence, compassion is essential to *human relationships* and to a fulfilled humanity. It is the path to enlightenment, and indispensable to the creation of a just economy and a peaceful global community.[9]

I have learned over the last few years that real compassion, like any of the other virtues, cannot be feigned. Though we needn't master the virtue before we experience it, being honest and sincere is essential. It's precisely the desire for it that will cause it to grow and expand, for it will shape our thoughts and actions. Where desire, need, and belief converge, beautiful things will happen. I have seen this in my own life and other's. Here is a firsthand observation I have witnessed countless times and almost always without failure.

I am the Patient Experience Coordinator at the hospital where I work. One of my responsibilities, among others, is to ensure that our patients are safe, well cared for clinically and emotionally, and that their needs (where realistic and possible) are met. That is a tall order and can be challenging some days.

So, I ask in my personal morning prayers to be led to those who need to be ministered to, who need to be listened to and heard, to be helped in a way that's meaningful for them.

When I do this, I am not disappointed. Something important happens. Sometimes it's the last person at the end of the day that I am visiting. I recognize at that moment this is the "one;" the person I was praying for. I too am enriched in the process and feel I played a small part in that person's recovery.

Everyone is our brother or sister. Everyone wants to be acknowledged, to be loved, to be listened to. Remember, compassion is the recognition and effort made to offer hope and relieve suffering.

"By [and through] compassion we make another's misery our own, and so by relieving them, we relieve ourselves as well."[10]

One of the biggest problems facing America's corporations today is employee disengagement. When employees are disengaged and not tuned in mentally, there is obviously a reduction in efficiency and production. Turnover increases as well. It costs money to train new people. The reason for a lack of engagement is usually multi-fold. It can be due to the lack of opportunity to advance or grow one's skills, having problems with one's manager, a lack of recognition, and a lack of meaning or purpose in what one is doing.

What has been found is when employees recognize opportunities to go out of their way and show care and kindness to others in the workplace, they feel a greater purpose and meaning in their work. There is a revitalization. It may be listening to a teammate vent as they struggle through a divorce. It might be taking the time to let an employee problem-solve a dilemma in the department that hasn't been fixed.

What Are the Fruits of Compassion?

Wangari Maathai was a renowned Kenyan social, environmental, and political activist and the first African woman to win the Nobel Peace Prize in 2004. She founded the Green Belt Movement, an environmental nongovernmental organization focused on the planting of trees, environmental conservation, and women's rights. She tells this moving story:

> Once there was a large forest fire and all the animals fled for their lives. They are all standing on the periphery of the forest, and watching the fire burn their homes. One of the animals looks up and sees a hummingbird flying to the lake, getting a beak full of water, and then dropping it on the fire. The animal says to the hummingbird, why are you doing this? There is no way you are going to put out the fire; to which the hummingbird replies, I know—but I am doing what I can![11]

> Often, when we see immeasurable suffering, we feel powerless or discouraged. But I tell you, each and every one of us has the capacity to make at least one person suffer less every day. So, go forth and do what you can.[12]

There is a tremendous feeling of gratitude in helping someone else. You are only one person, but we all know the power of one. Nearly every important cause or work ever undertaken began with an idea or a thought—that was then acted upon. Choose to consciously make a difference in the life of someone each day!

"If you want others to be happy, practice compassion. If you want to be happy, practice compassion."[13]

Purpose, peace, gratitude, and happiness, these are some of the fruits of compassion.

Conclusion

I can envision a modern-day renaissance, a spiritual one; one that supports the sisterhood and brotherhood of man's humanity to man, where each person truly cares and looks out for his neighbor. Are we not our "brother's keeper?" (Genesis 4:9).

This would happen if we taught and embraced divine, natural law. It once was taught as a general rule in the home, in the schools, and at church. Today, it would have to be established as vital and given proper attention. When virtues are learned and developed, they generate an internal change within the mind and heart, which produces certain happiness and contributes to a civil society. An interesting truth was offered many years ago by Ezra Taft Benson. He said,

> The Lord works from the inside out. The world works from the outside in. The world would take people out of the slums. Christ [and other godly influences] takes the slums out of people, and then they [would] take themselves out of the slums. The world would mold men by changing their environment. Christ [and other godly influences] changes [people], who then change their environment. The world would shape [human] behavior, but Christ [and other Godly influences] can change human nature" (Ezra Taft Benson, 1985).

Earlier, we recounted the story of the good Samaritan, whereby a certain lawyer challenged the Savior by asking Him what was necessary to inherit eternal life. Christ responded by asking him what was written in the law.

The lawyer knowing the law well, immediately replied, "Thou shalt love the Lord thy God with all thy heart, and with all thy soul, and with all thy strength, and with all thy mind; and thy neighbor as thyself."

After finishing the story and contrasting the actions of the good Samaritan with the priest and Levite, the Savior inquired, "'Which now of these three, thinkest thou, was neighbour unto him that fell among the thieves?' And he (the lawyer) said, 'He that shewed *mercy* [and compassion] on him.' Then said Jesus unto him,

'Go, and do thou likewise'" (Luke 10: 36–37).

What a tall task that is!

To love a stranger, to love more fully, deeply, and without condition.

The essence of this love is called charity or compassion, and it seeks to relieve the suffering of another. Is there anyone you know that isn't suffering? This kind of love is pure and unadulterated; it's the kind of love that God has for us.

If we decided to, loving others in this way would come slowly, here a little and there a little. Changing our minds isn't easy; changing our hearts is even harder. This is love of the highest order, a covenant kind of love. But it can happen.

Many have already walked this path. It will take many more to change the world. When we've experienced something and know it deep inside, we must honor it! When someone has been touched and changed in a deeper way, he or she will not be satisfied until they become a useful vessel in the hands of the Creator. (Remember Jean Valjean in that poignant moment with the priest in *Les Miserables*.)

Jeremiah records the Lord's words with the following, "I will put my [higher] law in their inward parts, and write it in their hearts" (Jeremiah 31:33).

That's when we'll be in partnership with God and experience Him more fully. And that's what it means, in part, when in the New Testament it says, "He is a new creature" (2 Corinthians 5:17).

At the end of the day, if the virtues we've practiced become a part of us, then we'll feel led in our efforts to make the world a better place. If we become fully intentional in our thoughts and actions, the world will be transformed.

Driving Change Deeper: An Action Plan

We learn and develop best when we practice!

Like Benjamin Franklin, try to focus on a few of these virtues each day. As you recite them in an affirmational way, they will become a part of you.

You can review them in the morning, before bed, or as part of a meditation anytime you wish.

It's been found that anything we do with repetition strengthens neural pathways. Any desire accompanied with repeated thought—drives and shapes behavior! Bottom line: the more you focus on your goals, the greater the likelihood they will become a reality. You'll begin to think, feel and act in those desired ways.

As you recite these virtues regularly, they will sink deep into your consciousness. They'll become a part of you. They will take root and ultimately bear fruit.

For as he thinketh in his heart, so is he. (Proverbs 23:7)

Remember, watch your thoughts, they become words; watch your words, they become your actions; watch your actions they become your habits; watch your habits they become your character; watch your character, it becomes your destiny. (Lao Tzu)

I have come up with a method that will help make these virtues penetrate in a greater way. Let me explain. Many religions in the world use prayer beads. The beads act as a tool to help the mind to focus.

In a similar way, this tool (string of beads) will help you to practice and enhance the twelve virtues. They are not religious emblems, but intended as a symbol for helping to imbed the desired principles. I have added a silver bead that represents our true beginnings, that we are all children of God with a destiny. I conclude the virtue beads with a gold bead that suggests we try to find someone to help each day, reminding us of the Golden Rule.

Using this tool repetitively creates a link between your senses (sight and touch) and the positive mental images (virtue beliefs) you wish to magnify. Practicing this over time will assist in deepening the virtues within you.

- Start with the gold bead and work your way through each of the others. *As you touch or rub each bead*, focus on the meaning of the words, thoughts, and ideas associated with that virtue. You can go through each of them in linear fashion.

You can do these as part of a daily ritual (morning, night, or whenever) or carry them around in your pocket and focus on them as you want or need. You can wear them as a bracelet or keep them in a handy place, where you do your affirmations.

I wish you well in this endeavor, if you're patient and pursue this faithfully, you'll not be disappointed, I assure you!

The Fruits of Virtue Affirmations

The Virtues of Belief

Hope—I believe that the world is full of good. Each moment, every day, presents limitless opportunities for learning and growth from the disappointments of life. Just as the sun and warmth return each spring, so will joy and peace be mine again.

- **"I will hold onto hope when times are tough; I will encourage others who lack hope."**

Faith—There is a"divine power" in the universe that is interested in my life. He is the Father of my spirit and will lead me along and buoy me up during moments of difficulty and despair. I need only call upon, and place my trust in Him.

- **"I have faith things will work out. He will help me when I reach out to him."**

Wisdom—As I learn from my experiences, I gain knowledge. As I reflect on that knowledge, I recognize truth that emanates from the infinite. I understand that aligning my life with virtue and the principles of natural law will bear much fruit.

- **"I will continually seek knowledge and wisdom, and be teachable in the the things I need to learn."**

The Virtues of Sacrifice

Humility—Though I am talented, unique, and special, many others have contributed to my health, success, and well-being. We all stand on the backs of giants. Everyone is as important as another. I am blessed beyond measure.

- **"There but for the grace of God go I; I need you/you need me, we both need God."**

Repentance—When I make a mess of my life, I will seek to make changes that will help me get better; I will follow the necessary steps and have peace of conscience restored.

- **"I will take responsibility for error and wrongdoing. I choose to grow and change and become the best version of myself."**

Patience—It's a virtue! Failing, suffering, enduring; all are a universal part of life and its struggle. Everyone participates. As I open myself to life's lessons, I will learn to be still and know that God is near.

- **"I will 'be still,' listen; and realize his plan for me will be revealed in time. "**

The Virtues of Character

Morality—There are principles of right and wrong ordained by the Maker Himself. Learning about these principles or natural law, will help me to know the path of peace and joy.

- **"I will seek to understand true principles, virtue and natural law, they are the blueprint of our universe."**

Self-mastery—The purpose of life is to learn and practice the laws and principles of virtue. Gaining strength of character requires great effort and a confidence that "the course of life being pursued [is trustworthy] and according to His will" (Joseph Smith, Third lecture on faith).

- **"I choose to develop virtue in my life—it results in peace and joy, and serves to strengthen my identity and character."**

Courage—This is a blend of compassion, justice, and self-mastery. I can choose love over fear. I am willing to take a stand for my convictions and do the right thing. There is a time and place for everything.

- "I can stand up, lean in and speak out, especially in a cause that's just!"

The Virtues of Love

Forgiveness—I choose to forgive and let go. When I forgive myself and others, I give myself some of the greatest gifts of all: peace, hope and happiness. In forgiving, I experience greater health and well-being in all its forms.

- "I choose to forgive—to be set free; then follows the promised blessings of peace and joy."

Gratitude—Everything I have is a gift. I am blessed beyond measure. I will look for the hand of God in my life, then realize more fully the abundance that surrounds me.

- "I am thankful for _____________. I count myself rich when considering all of my blessings."

Compassion—Loving others through relieving another's suffering is one of the great lessons and privileges of life. When I serve in this way, I find great peace and satisfaction. I can serve like "the lady with the lamp" (Florence Nightingale).

- "I will choose to help someone in distress, for they are part of our human family."

Notes

Hope

1 Rohr, Richard; *Preparing for Christmas*, Franciscan Media, (September 10, 2012.

2 Graves, Dan; MSL; Christianity.com https://www.christianity.com/church/church-history/timeline/1701-1800/did-robert-robinson-wander-as-he-feared-11630313.html

3 Hindmarsh, Bruce; *Was He Too Prone to Wander*, Desiring God; June 16, 2019.

4 Robinson, Robert; hymn written in 1758; hymnary.org/text/come_thou_fount_of_every_blessing

5 Shel Silverstein, *Where the Sidewalk Ends*, HarperCollins Publishers, New York, NY, 1974.

6 Orison Swett Marden

7 (Franklin, Benjamin; 'The Autobiography of Benjamin Franklin, Plan for Attaining Moral Perfection, chapter 9, Penguin Books, New York, NY, 1986).

8 Ibid

9 Callahan, Steven, as told to Mike Peake, *"Experience: I was adrift on a raft in the Atlantic for 76 days."* The Guardian, 23 Mar 2012)

10 Ibid

11 Callahan, Steven; *Adrift: Seventy-six Days Lost at Sea*, Mariner Books, 2002

12 Nietzsche

Faith

1 Esahe, Nylse; Lifenotes, Oct. 15, 2018, https://www.lifenotesencouragement.com/2018/10/hopeandfaith.html

2 Nelson, Russel M., "An Especially Noble Calling," interview with Joy D Jones, April 2020 General Conference, the Church of Jesus Christ of Latter day Saints.

3 New Testament, James 2:14–18.

4 Herbert Benson, *VHL Family Forum* 5:4, December 1997.

5 (attributed to Thomas Aquinas, most likely a loose paraphrase of things he taught.)

6 Herbert Benson, VHL Family Forum 5:4, Dec.1997.

7 (New Testament, Mark 16:17–18)

8 Jenkins, Dallas; director of "The Chosen," a mini-series on life of Christ; *Creators of VidAngels The Chosen to film second season in Utah*; Deseret news, 8/19/20.

9 Vertical Worship, song *Faithful Now,* found on YouTube, premiered feb 28, 2020.

10 Alma 32: 21

11 Scott Schieman. Socioeconomic Status and Beliefs about God's Influence in Everyday Life. *Sociology of Religion*, 2010; DOI: 10.1093/socrel/srq004

12 Barack Obama, fundraising speech for the presidency in San Francisco, Barack Obama, April/2008.

13 Romans 10: 14

Wisdom

1 Socrates

2 *Albert Einstein to J. Dispentiere—March 24, 1954. AEA 59-495*

3 (*Knowledge vs Wisdom*, PhiloScifi, Posted on 9/26/2010 by Justarius) https://philoscifi.com/2010/09/26/knowledge-vs-wisdom/

4 Matthew 5:48

5 2 Nephi 28: 30

6 1 Kings 3:3–15, 28 KJV (underlined words were provided for emphasis)

7 Gottfredson, Linda S. (1997). "Mainstream Science on Intelligence (editorial)" (PDF). *Intelligence*. 24: 13–23. doi:10.1016/s0160-2896(97)90011-8. ISSN 0160-2896. Archived (PDF) from the original on 22 December 2014.

8 Neisser, Ulrich; Boodoo, Gwyneth; Bouchard, Thomas J.; Boykin, A. Wade; Brody, Nathan; Ceci, Stephen J.; Halpern, Diane F.; Loehlin, John C.; Perloff, Robert; Sternberg, Robert J.; Urbina, Susana (1996). "Intelligence: Knowns and unknowns"(PDF). *American Psychologist*. 51 (2): 77–101. doi:10.1037/0003-066x.51.2.77. ISSN 0003-066X. Archived (PDF) from the original on 28 March 2016. Retrieved 9 October 2014.

9 Goleman, D. (1998). Working with Emotional Intelligence. New York: Bantam Books

10 Vaughn, Frances; "What is Spiritual Intelligence"?; Journal of Humanistic Psychology; Vol. 42, Issue 2, April 2, 2002, pp. 16–33.

11 Ibid

12 Atkinson, M. (2012) *Discover true happiness.* The power of spiritual intelligence

13 Pratt, Parley P., *Key to the Science of Theology*, 9th ed. [1965], p. 101

14 2 Nephi 9:28–29, 42

15 Doctrine & Covenants 46: 8–9, 26

16 Mosiah 2:17

17 The Church of Jesus Christ of Latter-day Saints, *Man's Search for Happiness,* movie created for the 1964 World's Fair held in New York, NY.)

18 James 3:17–18

Humility

1 Barrie, J.M., *The Little Minister,* Fenno and Company, 1891.

2 Hemingway, Ernest, *The Wild Years,* Dell Publishing, 1967.

3 Joseph Prince, *Unmerited Favor,* published by Charisma House, 2009

4 Martin Buber

5 Sorensen, Ted. "*Counselor: A Life at the Edge of History;* Sorenson reported he got the phrase from "the regional chamber of commerce, the New England Council, and used it in talks for President Kennedy; New York: HarperCollins Publishers, 2008. Page 227.

6 Benson, Ezra Taft, *Beware of Pride,* General Conference of The Church of Jesus Christ of Latter-day Saints, April 1989.

7 Lewis, C. S., *Mere Christianity*, New York: Macmillan, 1952, pp.109–110.

8 Doctrine and Covenants 121: 39

9 Proverbs 16: 18

10 Katerina Stoykova Klemer

11 David Brooks, *The Road to Character*, Random House, 2015.

12 Lincoln, Abraham; *First Inaugural Address*, March 1861.

13 Batterson, Mark, *The Circle Maker,* Zondervan, 2016.

14 Alma, Ch. 23–24

15 Warren, Rick, *The Purpose Driven Life*, Zondervan, 2002

16 Matthew 5:3–16

17 Matthew 8:4

18 Matthew 26: 53

19 Acts 10:38

20 Phillipians 4: 7

Repentance

1 Eliot, Goerge; *Daniel DeRonda;* Henneberry & Co. January 1, 1890.

2 Lee, Harper; *To Kill a Mockingbird,* J P Lippincott, 1960.

3 Pink, Arthur; *Studies On Saving Faith;* Lulu Press, Inc, 2013.

4 Alma 41: 10

5 Uchtdorf, Dieter F., *A Matter of a Few Degrees;* General Conference of the Church of Jesus Christ of Latter day Saints; April/2008.

6 Watson, Thomas; *The Doctrine of Repentance,* 1668.

7 Ibid

8 2 Corinthians 5: 17

9 Ezekiel 11:19

10 2 Nephi 28:7–8, 21–22

11 Homer, The Odyssey

12 Jenkins, Dave; *What Does Christianity Mean in the Bible,* Christianity.com, 2020.
https://www.christianity.com/wiki/christian-terms/what-does-transgression-mean-in-the-bible.html

13 Gandhi, Mahatma; *The Gandhi Reader: A Sourcebook of His Life and Writings,* Grove Press, 1994, P-194.

14 Scott, Richard G., *Peace of Concscience, Peace of Mind,* General Conference, October/2004.

15 Hebrews 12:11

16 Alma 13: 13

Patience

1 George Saville

2 Millman, Dan, *"The Life You Were Born To Live,"* H J Kramer, 1993, P-394.

3 Updike, John

4 Wallace, Cynthia; granted permission to share, as posted on her Facebook page.

5 Becca lee

6 Benjamin Franklin

7 Tony Gaskins

Morality

1 de Tocqueville, Alexis, *Democracy in America,* University of Chicago Press, 2002.

2 Ibid

3 Haidt, Jonathon, *The Righteous Mind: Why Good People are Divide by Politics and Religion;* Pantheon Books, 2012.

4 *Boy Scouts of America Membership Controversies,* Wikipedia https://en.wiki pedia.org/wiki/Boy_Scouts_of_America_membership_controversies

5 Soave, Robby, "Study: 80% of Americans Believe Political Correctness Is a Problem; Reason: Free Minds and Free Markets, 19/11/2018.

6 Paine, Thomas, Agrarian Justice (phamplet), 1797 in english.

7 Dissani, Rishabh R., Values and Principles, February 12, 2016.
https://dazne.net/vp/

8 Hemingway, Ernest, Death in the Afternoon, Publisher: Charles Scribner Sons, 1932

9 https://www.apocryphicity.ca/2018/07/08/the-gnostic-pinocchio/

8 de Tocqueville, Alexis; quoting Michel Montaigne in; *Democracy in America,* Publishers: Saunders & Otley, London, 1835-40.

9 Unmin, J D; Sex and Culture; Oxford University Press; London, 1934

10 Toynbee, Arnold; Study of History, Oxford Press, 1934-1961

11 Gibbon, Edward; *History of the Decline and Fall of the Roman Empire;* Steven & Caddell, London, 1776–89.

12 J.G.A. Pocock, "Between Machiavelli and Hume: Gibbon as Civic Humanist and Philosophical Historian," *Daedalus* 105:3 (1976), 153–169; and in Further reading: Pocock, *The Enlightenments of Edward Gibbon, 1737–1764,* 303–304; *The First Decline and Fall,* 304–306.

13 Alcorn, Randy; *Immorality and Cultural Decline; Eternal Perspective Ministeries,* 2/1/1993. https://www.epm.org/resources/1993/Feb/1/immorality-cultural -decline/

14 Percy Bysshe Shelley, *"Ozymandias,"* in *Miscellaneous and Posthumous Poems of Percy Bysshe Shelley,* London: W. Benbow, 1826; 100.

Self-mastery

1 Bodhidharma

2 McKay, Brett and Katie; *Lessons in Manliness: Benjamin Franklin in Pursuit of the Virtuous Life,* Feb 24, 2008.

https://www.artofmanliness.com/articles/lessons-in-manliness-benjamin -franklins-pursuit-of-the-virtuous-life/

3 Alfred Lord Tennyson

4 Epictetus

5 These wise words are attributed to Lao Tzu, and are now believed to be "a compilation of Taoist sayings by many hands." Lao Tzu was an ancient Chinese philosopher and reputed author of the Tao Te Ching, the founder of philosophical Taoism.

6 Smith, Joseph; *Teachings of the Prophet Joseph Smith, p. 304.*

7 Wheatley, Jack and Lois, (their life), *The Roots of Generosity,* BYU Magazine, Winter 2013 Issue.

8 Ibid

9 Ibid

Courage

1 Maya Angelou. *Maya Angelou: A Glorious Celebration;* Doubleday, 2008, p-277.

2 Jeanette Coron

3 Brown, Brene, *Rising Strong,* Random House, 2015.

4 Hilton, Whitney; granted permission to share; and as reported on her Facebook page.

5 Doss, Desmond Jr., *Hacksaw Ridge, Interview with Desmond Doss, Jr.;* Military .com, 4 Nov 2016.

https://www.military.com/video/off-duty/movies/hacksaw-ridge-interview -desmond-doss-jr/5196860814001

6 John 15: 13

7 George D. Seymour (May 2006). *Documentary Life of Nathan Hale: Comprising All Available Official and Private Documents Bearing on the Life of the Patriot.* Kessinger Publishing. ISBN 978-1-4286-0043-0. Retrieved October 17, 2010, p-310.

8 Buxton, Peter; *Tuskegee Truth Teller,* told by Carl Elliot, The American Scholar, December 4, 2017.

9 Presser, Lizzie, *The Black American Amputation Epidemic,* the story of Dr. Foluso Fakorede's mission to save patients legs and lives; ProPublica, May 19, 2020

https://features.propublica.org/diabetes-amputations/black-american-ampu tation-epidemic/

10 William G T Shedd

Gratitude

1 Anonymous

2 Bryne, Rhonda; *The Secret,* Atria Books, 2006.

3 *Awakenings,* the movie; starring Robin Williams, Robert DeNiro

4 Buscaglia, Leo; *"Born for Love: Reflections on Loving,"* (attributed to a Buddhist teacher Leo had while living in Thailand), Ballantine Books, 1994.

5 John Updike

Forgiveness

1 "What Is Forgiveness?, The Greater Good Science Center at the University of California, Berkeley; 2020; https://greatergood.berkeley.edu/topic/forgiveness/ definition

2 Corrie ten boom

3 Mason Cooley

4 King, Martin Luther Jr.; *A Gift of Love,* Beacon Press, Nov/2012.

5 Lewis, C. S., *In letters to Malcom, Chiefly on Prayer*, Geoffrey Bles Pub., 1964.

6 Les Brown

7 Tullis, Paul; *"Can Forgiveness Play a Role in Criminal Justice,"* story of Sujatha Baliga; NY Times Magazine, , January 4, 2013

8 Ibid

9 *Forgiveness Without Conditions,* story of Charles Roberts—Amish School shooter; Diocesan, August 16, 2018.

https://diocesan.com/forgiveness-without-conditions/

10 Green, John; *Looking for Alaska,* Penguin Books, 2005.

11 Lincoln, Abraham; *Second Inaugural address*; 4 March 1965

Compassion

1 Luke 10:25–37

2 McPherson, Miller; Smith-Lovin, Lynn; Brashears, Matthew E.; *Social Isolation in America: Changes in Core Discussion Networks Over Two Decades*, American Sociological Review, June 1, 2006

3 Plato

4 Hilton, Whitney; eye witness account of Utah nurse who helped in the NYC hospitals during the 2020 pandemic

5 Schopenhauer, Arthur, *Ueber die Grundlage der Moral*, 1840; *On the Basis of Morality.* Translated by E.F.J. Payne. Providence : Berghahn Books. ISBN 1-57181-053-6, 1995.

6 *"Pray for coach Sloan," Karl Malone urges panel of NBA legends from the 1990s;* Sean Walker, KSL.com., May 17, 2020 . https://www.ksl.com/article/46754378/pray-for-coach-sloan-karl-malone -urges-panel-of-nba-legends-from-the-1990s

7 Zaki, Jamil; *Kindness Contagion*, Scientific American, July 26, 2016

8 Mother Teresa

9 Armstrong, Karen; *The Charter for Compassion.* Archived 10 May 2011 at the Wayback Machine

10 Sir Thomas Browne

11 Doty, Dr James; *Centrality of Compassion in Human Life and Society*, story told by Wangarī Maathai to Dr Doty, who then shared it with the audience during the Dalai Lama address at Stanford University; October 14, 2010

12 Doty, Dr James; *Centrality of Compassion in Human Life and Society*, closing remarks shared with the audience during the address by the Dalai Lama at Stanford University; October 14, 2010

13 Dalai Lama